MODERN EUROPEAN PHILOSOPHY

Editors
ALAN MONTEFIORE, BALLIOL COLLEGE, OXFORD
HIDE ISHIGURO, COLUMBIA UNIVERSITY
RAYMOND GEUSS, PRINCETON UNIVERSITY

MEINONG AND THE PRINCIPLE OF INDEPENDENCE

T0382569

MEINONG
AND THE PRINCIPLE OF
INDEPENDENCE

ITS PLACE IN
MEINONG'S THEORY OF OBJECTS
AND ITS SIGNIFICANCE IN
CONTEMPORARY PHILOSOPHICAL LOGIC

KAREL LAMBERT

Professor of Philosophy,
University of California at Irvine

CAMBRIDGE UNIVERSITY PRESS

CAMBRIDGE

LONDON   NEW YORK   NEW ROCHELLE

MELBOURNE   SYDNEY

CAMBRIDGE UNIVERSITY PRESS
Cambridge, New York, Melbourne, Madrid, Cape Town, Singapore, São Paulo, Delhi

Cambridge University Press
The Edinburgh Building, Cambridge CB2 8RU, UK

Published in the United States of America by Cambridge University Press, New York

www.cambridge.org
Information on this title: www.cambridge.org/9780521271998

© Cambridge University Press 1983

First published 1983
Re-issued in this digitally printed version 2009

A catalogue record for this publication is available from the British Library

Library of Congress Catalogue Card Number: 82 – 23628

ISBN 978-0-521-25085-6 hardback
ISBN 978-0-521-27199-8 paperback

Für den Hirschverfolger und Herrn Koch,
und die Familie Michelitsch

CONTENTS

EDITORS' INTRODUCTION

The purpose of this series is to help to make contemporary European philosophy intelligible to a wider audience in the English-speaking world, and to suggest its interest and importance, in particular to those trained in analytical philosophy. The first book in the series was, appropriately enough, Charles Taylor's book *Hegel and Modern Society*. It is by reference to Hegel that one may indicate most starkly the difference between the two traditions to whose intercommunication the series seeks to contribute; for the analytical philosophy of the contemporary Anglo-Saxon world was largely developed by Moore, Russell, and others in revolt against idealism and the influence of British Hegelians at the turn of this century. It is true that the British and American idealists had themselves already diverged considerably from Hegel, but their holistic philosophy was certainly Hegelian both in terminology and in aspiration. Moore and Russell, for their part, obviously owed most to a different tradition, one stemming from Hume. Nevertheless, it should not be forgotten that they too were influenced by European contemporaries, to whose writings, indeed, they explicitly appealed in their revolt against the British Hegelians. In particular they admired two European philosophers who had very little sympathy for Hegelianism: Brentano in the case of Moore, and in the case of Russell, Frege.

The next book in our series, Raymond Geuss's *The Idea of a Critical Theory*, discussed issues which could be understood only by reference back to the thought of Hegel and Marx, which – in marked contrast to what happened in the English-speaking world – was absorbed and further developed, in their own characteristic ways, by the main trends of radical thought on the European continent. In England, on the other hand, philosophical opposition to 'Establishment' ways of thinking and patterns of influence was developed in opposition to Hegel rather than under his influence. In the mid-thirties, just when Hegel's philosophy was being introduced seriously to the academic world in Paris, A. J. Ayer returned from Vienna to Oxford as a champion of the logical positivism of the Vienna Circle, whose chief target of attack was precisely Hegel. It is true that logical positivism was short-lived in England; and even in the United States, to which several members of the Vienna Circle eventually escaped, it represented an important phase rather than a lasting school. But many of the philosophical virtues with which it was most concerned continued to be fostered. What is now called analytical philosophy, with its demand for thoroughness of conceptual analysis and its suspicion of rhetoric and grandiose structures, came to be more and more dominant in the English-speaking world. The philosophical attitude which it represents and which distinguishes it from the dominant European schools of thought is succinctly expressed in the foreword to the *Philosophical Remarks* (1930) of Wittgenstein, whose influence on analytical philosophy was incalculable:

This spirit is different from the one which informs the vast stream of European and American civilization in which all of us stand. The one spirit expresses itself in an onwards movement, in building ever larger and more complicated structures: the other in striving after clarity and perspicacity in no matter what structure... And so the first adds one construction to another, moving on and up, as it were, from one stage to the next, while the other remains where it is and what it tries to grasp is always the same.

Like Brentano, whose pupil he was, Meinong was, as Professor Lambert notes, much esteemed by both Moore and Russell, and his work has been a source of stimulus to a number of more recent leading analytic philosophers. Nevertheless, it would not be unfair to say that not only is such a positive appreciation of his work not very widespread, but that there is in general among analytic philosophers still only a very limited knowledge of its actual nature. In this book Professor Lambert is primarily concerned to elucidate and to defend Meinong's famous principle of the independence of the nature of objects (their *Sosein*) from whatever being (*Sein*) that they may or may not possess. He is able to show the great interest that this principle must have for anyone concerned with the problems of philosophical logic, in particular for those concerned with theories of predication and quantification. We are given a vigorous defence of free logics – that is to say, with logics free of existence assumptions with respect to their terms, general and singular, and different from standard quantification theory belonging to the tradition of Frege, Tarski, or Quine. We are shown where Professor Lambert's own version of free logic differs from the position of Meinong, and where it coincides with it. Indeed, so closely does Professor Lambert involve Meinong in these debates that one may well be led to wonder whether the so-called distinction between analytical and continental philosophy has any clear or useful application to his case at all.

But everyone knows, of course, that the labels 'analytical' and 'continental' are in many ways very unsatisfactory. There are philosophers of the phenomenological tradition working in the United States, though very few in the field of philosophy of mathematics. There are many other philosophers engaged in work of conceptual analysis in the Scandinavian countries, Poland, and (more recently) Germany. Moreover, the universities of Europe which have not been influenced by the analytical tradition – and these include nearly all of those in France and Italy, and the great majority of those in German-speaking countries and in Eastern Europe – have themselves by no means represented any unitary tradition. The disagreements or even lack of communication between, for instance, Hegelians, Marxists, phenomenologists and Thomists have often been deep. But these disagreements are 'small' in comparison with the barriers of mutual ignorance and distrust between the main representatives of the analytical tradition on the one hand and the main philosophical schools of the European continent of the other (schools which are also dominant in Latin America, Japan, and even some universities in the United States and Canada). These barriers are inevitably reinforced by the fact that, until very recently at any rate, even the best students from the universities situated on either side have tended to emerge from their studies with such divergent areas of knowledge and ignorance, competence and incompetence, that they are hardly equipped even to enter into informed discussion with each other about the nature of what separates them.

We tend, nevertheless, to forget that the erection of these barriers is a relatively recent phenomenon. Brentano, writing on the philosophy of mind at the end of the last century, made frequent reference to J. S. Mill and to other contemporary British philosophers. In turn, as we have noticed, Moore refers to Brentano. Bergson discusses William James frequently in his works. For Husserl one of the most important philosophers was Hume. The thinkers discussed seriously by Russell include not only Frege and Poincaré, but also Meinong. How unfortunate, then, that those who have followed in their footsteps have refused to read or to respect one another, the one group convinced that the other survives on undisciplined rhetoric and an irresponsible lack of rigour, the other suspecting the former of aridity, superficiality, and over-subtle trivialization.

The books of this series represent contributions by philosophers who have worked in the analytical tradition but who now tackle problems specifically raised by philosophers of the main traditions to be found within contemporary Europe. They are works of philosophical argumentation and of substance rather than merely introductory résumés. We believe that they may contribute towards the formation of a richer and less parochial framework of thinking, a wider frame within which mutual criticism and stimulation will be attempted and where mutual disagreements will at least not be based on ignorance, contempt or distortion.

PREFACE

This little book is not intended as a contribution to Meinongian scholarship. Indeed, when the editors of the series in which it now appears first approached me about doing an essay on Meinong's thought, I declined, pleading insufficient scholarly expertise – there are after all, others much more informed than I about the character and detail of Meinong's thought. But when the editors responded that their intention was not primarily to present a set of scholarly essays on the thought of various continental philosophers, but rather to publish a series exploring the bearing on contemporary analytic philosophy of some part or feature of the doctrine of those same continental figures, I reconsidered and accepted their kind invitation to contribute an essay on perhaps the most widely known aspect of Meinong's philosophy, the principle that being so (*Sosein*) is independent of being (*Sein*).

A few remarks about the goals of this book should be made. The major goal is to examine the effect of the principle of the independence of being so from being on the theory of predication, with special attention to Meinong's (often reconstructed) approach to this topic, and thence on some contemporary developments in philosophical logic. I am aware that a discussion involving in part what the late Aubrey Castell called 'the aridities of logic' may not hold out the promise of much excitement to many. But for me, the line between metaphysics and logic has always been continuous, and the philosophical excitement evoked by the former does not diminish when the border is crossed to the latter. At any rate a discussion concerning analytic philosophy sooner or later gets snarled in logical matters; discussing analytic philosophy without touching on logic is like trying to discuss empirical science without mentioning experiments.

One will not find in these pages a griceful[1] piece of philosophical analysis though the overall effort falls pretty clearly in that part of philosophical no-man's-land closer to the analytic side. Certainly it is not at all in the spirit of the 'back to the text' movement so popular in some European quarters today. This new brand of philosophical evangelism is deplorable. It is about as illuminating as the literalist reading of the Bible favored by religious fundamentalists of the southern United States. I personally doubt whether even a person's literal remarks about the weather can hope to survive logical collapse, to 'deconstruct', without some (charitable) inferences about his intentions and what he really meant.

A great deal of this slim volume is unabashedly speculative, though I hope not too outlandish nor overly impressionistic. Great effort has gone into writing a book that is intended to appeal, at least in parts (and perhaps as a whole), to a wider range of interests than is normally that of the audience of Anglo-American philosophers. The degree to which this goal is successfully met is, of course, left up to the reader's judgment (though I wish it weren't).

Let me briefly recount the salient features in each of the six chapters of this book. In the Introduction an effort is made to say why Meinong's work is important, that it is not merely interesting as an historical stage in (as they say on television) 'the continuing drama' that is philosophy, but is rather a compendium of valuable and ingenious ideas bearing directly on some of the most central and profound issues of contemporary analytic philosophy – and by 'contemporary' I mean within the last two decades. In the second chapter Meinong's theory of objects (*Gegenstandstheorie*) is sketched, along with motivations, comparisons with the views of other philosophers, and most importantly a logical representation of the famous prin-

---

[1] See the entry 'Griceful', in *The Philosophical Lexicon* (editor in chief, D. Dennett), The American Philosophical Association, 1978.

ciple of the independence of being so from being. There is a
discussion of the central place of this principle in the Meinongian world picture, and a clarification of the difference
between it and a principle with which it is often confused, the
principle of the indifference of the pure object to being.

The third chapter deals with Meinong's theory of predication and the bearing of the principle of independence on it.
Predication is construed as a kind of logical form and logical
form, following David Kaplan, is identified with a way of
assessing a statement for truth-value. The principle of
independence is interpreted as lifting a constraint inherent in
the traditional view of predication having a core principle
shared by Meinong, Russell, and a reformist Frege. The fate of
Meinong's nontraditional view of predication, when examined
in the light of his doctrine of beingless objects, is discussed,
and the sense in which Meinong's theory of predication is nonextensional is detailed.

In the fourth chapter the connection between the principle
of independence and predication is further examined. A different theory of predication is outlined, a theory congenial
with the views of some modified Meinongians, free logicians,
and Quine. The underlying theory of logical form reflected in
the traditional theory of predication and in Meinong's own
theory, and discussed in the previous chapter, is challenged,
and the essential independence of the principle of independence from the alternative theory of predication is discussed.
The alternative theory is proved to be nonextensional.

Chapter 5 is a philosophical introduction to free logic and
the relation of the principle of independence to the various
versions of it. It is seen to be a decisive principle in the development of free logic, and its relevance to the judgment of which
version of free logic is philosophically the most adequate is
shown. It is argued that the different versions of free logic are
indeed dependent on different theories of predication but have
less to do with the core of those theories than with an important constraint on them. Chapter 6, the final chapter, is a
prolonged defense of the principle of independence and its im-

mediate consequences, especially those having to do with predication.

There are many to thank in the development and writing of this essay. Much of the research for it was done while I was a Fulbright Hayes Senior Fellow at the University of Salzburg in 1980, and during the summer of 1979 when part of my efforts were underwritten by a National Endowment for the Humanities Summer Stipend. To both programs I am much indebted. Thanks are also due to the Universitetsforlaget, publishers of the journal *Inquiry*, for permission to reprint parts of the essay 'On the Philosophical Foundations of Free Logic' (*Inquiry*, 24/ 2 (1981)) in Chapter 5. In a more personal vein my debts are essentially to five persons. To Rheinhard Fabian of the Karl-Franzens Universität, Graz, for bringing to my attention some valuable unpublished work in the Meinong archives; to James Hearne for letting me see part of his forthcoming translation of Meinong's *Über Annahmen* (2nd edn); to Ermanno Bencivenga and Terence Parsons for their helpful and kind comments on the penultimate draft of this essay; and most of all to my friend and colleague, Edgar Morscher, of the University of Salzburg. He is surely among the most knowledgeable scholars in the world on Meinong, Brentano, and Bolzano, and I owe him very much, not least for his determination to keep me on the straight and narrow path. Alas, there are limits to the effectiveness even of the most (goodnaturedly) determined and honest people.

Finally, I am very grateful to Mandy Macdonald for her suggestions as to improvements in style.

Laguna Niguel, California   Karel Lambert

INTRODUCTION: THE RELEVANCE OF MEINONG'S VIEWS TO CONTEMPORARY PHILOSOPHY

The opinion still persists in Anglo-American analytic philosophy that Alexius Meinong, though undeniably imaginative and visionary, could not keep clear the line between fantasy and philosophy. Yet Meinong's ideas were not the result of unrestrained speculation. Nor was the source of their inspiration very different from that occasioning the views of the most hard-headed analytic philosophers. On the former point there is the testimony of Russell himself, who, in his sensitive study, 'Meinong's Theory of Assumptions and Complexes', wrote:

I wish to emphasise the admirable method of Meinong's researches, which, in a brief epitome, it is quite impossible to preserve. Although empiricism as a philosophy does not appear to be tenable, there is an empirical manner of investigating, which should be applied in every subject-matter. This is possessed in a very perfect form by the works we are considering. A frank recognition of the data, as inspection reveals them, precedes all theorising; when a theory is propounded, the greatest skill is shown in the selection of facts favourable or unfavourable, and in eliciting all relevant consequences of the facts adduced. There is thus a rare combination of acute inference with capacity for observation. The method of philosophy is not fundamentally unlike that of other sciences: the differences seem to be only in degree. The data are fewer, but are harder to apprehend; and the inferences required are probably more difficult than in any other subject except mathematics. But the important point is that, in philosophy as elsewhere, there are self-evident truths from which we must start, and that these are discoverable by the process of inspection or observation, although the material to be observed is not, for the most part, composed of existent things. Whatever may ultimately prove to be the value of Meinong's particular contentions, the value of his method is undoubtedly very great; and on this account, if on no other, he deserves careful study.[1]

On the latter point there is, first, Meinong's own statement that grammar should (and did in his own case) play a major part in the development of the theory of objects:

However different the two cases may be on the whole, one is tempted to say that the general theory of Objects must learn from grammar just as the special theory of Objects must learn from mathematics.[2]

Second, there is the example of Meinong's masterful work, *Über Annahmen*.[3] In that provocative study of those proposition-like entities he called *Objektive* (objectives), he grounds many of his major claims essentially on a linguistic analysis of what Russell would later call 'propositional attitudes' discourse.

Moreover, his theory of beingless objects is startling only against a deliberately impoverished background, one that ignores, for example, modal discourse. This is a fashionable attitude in certain circles nowadays based on philosophical skepticism concerning the most common and widely promulgated foundations for such discourse – the possible worlds account – a skeptical tradition beginning with Russell early in this century and reaching full bloom in Quine's writings. It may be true, as Quine has suggested,[4] that the admission into one's ontology of objects clawing their way toward actuality tends to weaken resistance to objects that cannot in principle so aspire, for instance Mill's immortal round square. But it is also true that the feeling of undisciplined ontic indulgence accompanying the postulation of such entities is in large part produced by belief in the sanctity of a certain canonical idiom,

---

[1] *Mind* NS 13 (1904), p. 205.
[2] A. Meinong, 'On the Theory of Objects', in R. M. Chisholm (ed.), *Realism and the Background of Phenomenology*, (The Free Press, New York, 1960), p. 103.
[3] Meinong, *Über Annahmen*, Barth, Leipzig, 1902.
[4] *Methods of Logic* (revised edition; Holt-Dryden, New York, 1959), pp. 201–2.

alleged to be adequate to the needs of science and philosophy, but in fact suffering from 'diminished capacity'. So once the background is expanded, once modal discourse and the like are included in the register of philosophically acceptable talk, as they should properly be, the move from unactualized possibles to unactualizable impossibles is not at all alarming. No doubt the inclination to think that one is talking, respectively, about the possible object *Pegasus* and the impossible object *the proof of the decidability of the full logic of predicates* in the statements

(1) Pegasus does not exist,

and

(2) The proof of the decidability of the full logic of predicates does not exist,

is as resistible as the inclination to think that one is talking about the thing *nothing* in the statement

(3) Nothing exists.

But the inclination is less easy to resist in modal statements such as

(4) Pegasus could not have existed,

and

(5) The proof of the decidability of the full logic of predicates can never exist.

And in the case of psychological and epistemic discourse – discourse expressing desires and needs on the one hand and what one knows on the other – the inclination to think that one is talking about nonexistent and even beingless objects is well-nigh overwhelming, as Terence Parsons has recently urged.[5] Though an ontology countenancing these objects may turn out to be wrong, it cannot be simply dismissed as wrongheaded.

Meinong's theory of objects thus becomes quite topical, a

[5] *Nonexistent Objects*, Yale University Press, New Haven, 1980.

theory that current analytic philosophers cannot in good con-
science or their own interest ignore out of hand. It is strange,
indeed, that Meinong was so highly esteemed by those two
giants of twentieth-century philosophy and major precursors
of the analytic movement, Russell and Moore, and so little ap-
preciated by generations of their followers. Lately the trend
has begun to shift, and Meinong's work, especially his theory
of objects, has attracted the attention of analytic philosophers
– Richard and Vivian Routley, Hector Castañeda, William
Rapaport, and Terence Parsons, to mention five of the most
current – though the philosophical importance of Meinong has
long been championed by John Findlay and Roderick
Chisholm.

Many of Meinong's ideas bear directly on topics of high
interest in the current analytic environment. Attention here
will be confined to four. First, Meinong's position on being
and nonbeing is especially relevant given the influence of
Quine's reflections on existence. In a recent if not widely
known essay on existence Quine affirms that he understands
'existence' to mean 'being' in .the widest sense of that word,
that he specifically eschews a narrow notion of existence
covering only a subset of the beings such as Russell employed
in *The Principles of Mathematics* and, as a matter of fact,
Meinong himself did in his theory of objects. (Meinong distinguished between subsistents and existents, and held the
latter to be a subclass of the former. But sometimes he says
confusingly that the subsistents as opposed to the existents are
timeless. The threat of inconsistency evaporates, however,
when one realizes that his contention is only that the *merely*
subsistent objects – those that have being but do not exist – are
timeless. Meinong's doctrine of subsistence and existence will
be further explained in the next chapter.) So much is explicit
in the following lines by Quine:

[Bergmann's] objection to equating existence with the values of the
variables turned on his taking the term 'existence', as philosophers
sometimes do, in a narrower sense than 'being' or 'subsistence'.
Russell once favored that terminology too, but it is not ... my

doctrine. What I equate with the values of the variables *is the broadest sense* of 'being' that the use of the variables is to be seen as accepting.[6]

Accordingly, Quine's conception of existence is essentially Meinong's conception of being or subsistence. Meinong thus emerges as Quine's natural philosophical adversary in both a general and a specific way. First, he rejects the general doctrine that the set of objects is identical with the set of existents (= beings, subsistents), a belief of which Quine is the foremost contemporary exponent. Second, he rejects the specific Quineian doctrine that to be is to be the value of a variable, as is plain from some of his quantificational assertions such as 'Every nonsubsistent object has properties', and 'There are non-subsistent objects'. Clearly these are quantifications over beingless objects. The reasons Meinong thought compelled admission of beingless objects are, therefore, of vital importance to those sharing Quine's predilections about existence, and, conversely, Quineian arguments in favor of the dictum that to be is to be the value of a variable can help the Meinong scholar assess the worth of Meinong's doctrine of beingless objects. Despite the mutual relevance and clarificational benefits latent in the Meinong–Quine opposition, apparently no Quineian on the current stage – including Quine himself – has shown any great interest in or awareness of Meinong's own arguments in favor of beingless objects.[7]

[6] W. V. Quine, 'Existence', in W. Yourgrau *et al.* (eds.), *Physics, Logic and History*, Plenum Press, New York, 1970; my italics.

[7] Reflection, and Terence Parsons' advice, compel mention of another interpretation of Quine's construal of existence. In this alternative construal 'existence' does not mean what Meinong means by 'being' but rather means what he means by 'object'. Thus, to say 'Pegasus exists' is to say 'There is an object that is Pegasus' (which is false for Quine but not for Meinong). This interpretation receives some support from Quine's remark in his famous essay 'On What There Is' (in L. Linsky (ed.), *Semantics and The Philosophy of Language*, University of Illinois, Urbana, 1952), where he abandons the word 'exists' and adopts the word 'is' for his ruminations on ontic commitment. A Meinongian might put this way of construing Quine as follows: 'Whereas "exists" and "being" have "significant contraries", "object" does not; whereas it makes sense to say "*x* does not exist" or "*x* has no being", it makes no sense at all to say "*x* is not an object", where *x* is a variable ranging over objects. Quine's view of "exists" is such that "*x* does not exist", like "*x* is not an obect", is not "significant". And indeed this seems to be justified by Quine's famous question "What exists?" and his response "Everything!", a question and response any

Second, another matter of considerable current interest on which Meinongian reflections might shed illumination concerns what are called, in recent discussions in the foundations of modal logic, 'Russellian singular propositions'. A singular proposition of the present kind, say, the singular proposition that this is white, contains as constituent the very *object*, the word 'this' specifies, rather than, say, an individual concept, in the position occupied by that object. This view of singular propositions is really Moore's, and was borrowed by Russell as early as 1904[8] It is *not* Russell's view in 'On Propositions: What They Are and How They Mean',[9] an essay most current discussion on the foundations of modal logic ignores. Now it has been argued by some that the correct explanation of truth in quantified modal logic requires singular propositions of the Moore–Russell kind. David Kaplan, for example, writes:

consider

(O) $(\exists x)\,(Fx \wedge \sim\Box Fx)$.

This sentence would not be taken by anyone to express a singular proposition. But in order to evaluate the truth-value of the component

$\Box Fx$

(under some assignment of an individual to the variable 'x'), we must first determine whether the *proposition* expressed by its component

Meinongian would agree with were the word "object" substituted for the word "exists".' On this alternative construal of Quine's conception of 'exists', Meinong could be expected to object in two ways. First, that the proposed convention for interpreting 'exists' is unwise because it casts traditional philosophical debates about existence in a misleading light. Thus when Meinong asserts 'There are impossible objects' it would be seriously misleading to say he holds impossible objects to exist. Or at the very least it is cumbersome to say they exist in one sense of the word, but do not in another (the spatio-temporal sense of 'exist'). Second, that what exists in this alternative construal is much greater than is dreamt of in Quine's philosophy; the things that qualify as objects (existents à la Quine) certainly exceed Quine's ontic catalogue.

[8] 'Meinong's Theory of Assumptions and Complexes', p. 206.
[9] In his *Logic and Knowledge* (ed. R. C. Marsh; Macmillan, New York, 1956), pp. 285–320.

F*x*

(under an assignment of an individual to the variable '*x*') is a necessary proposition. So in the course of analyzing (O), we are required to determine the proposition associated with a formula containing a *free* variable.[10]

To sum up, though a complex statement such as (O) may not itself *directly* presuppose appeal to singular propositions, the evaluation of it decomposes into the evaluation of its components, for example 'F*x*'. The evaluation of these rock-bottom components appeals directly to singular propositions. Thus, '*x*' in 'F*x*' refers to the object in the singular prop-proposition possessing what is stood for by the rest of 'F*x*', and these collections of objects and properties are directly involved in computing the truth-value of '□F*x*'.

What bearing do Meinong's ideas have on the connection between quantified modal logic and singular propositions? The answer lies in the following identification: Russell in 1904 explicitly *identifies* propositions of the Moore–Russell kind with those objects Meinong called *Objektive*.[11] So if quantified modal logic requires singular propositions of the Moore–Russell kind, it requires Meinongian objectives. Conversely, whatever support for Meinong's theory of objectives there may be transfers automatically to the foundations of modal logic under discussion here.

It must be admitted that the identification of singular propositions with 'singular' objectives is not uncontroversial. John Findlay has objected to Russell's equation in his splendid book, *Meinong's Theory of Objects and Values*.[12] But it may be questioned whether Findlay's complaints are really substantial given the misleading picture of a complex that he foists on Moore and Russell and which he says adequately represents the Moore–Russell view of the nature of propositions but not Meinong's conception of the nature of an objective. Further,

[10] D. Kaplan, 'Demonstratives' (unpublished manuscript, Draft No. 2, Philosophy Department, UCLA, Los Angeles, 1977), Preface.
[11] 'Meinong's Theory of Assumptions and Complexes', p. 206.
[12] Clarendon Press, Oxford, 1963; pp. 94–101.

Findlay's assimilation of Meinongian objectives that obtain to facts, as opposed to propositions, conflicts with his admission elsewhere that the truth-value vehicles for Meinong are often taken to be objectives. For facts, Findlay admits, are not strictly speaking the bearers of truth and falsity, though propositions are. At any rate, the parallel between singular propositions of the Moore–Russell kind and 'singular' objectives is so close that the theoretical light to be shed on the account of truth in modal logic championed by Kaplan and others such as Kit Fine cannot but be substantial. This observation is further conditioned by the fact that Meinong had much to say about objectives not only in the theory of objects but also, as earlier noted, in his superb opus, *Über Annahmen*.[13]

A third Meinongian notion of undeniable contemporary significance is his fundamental notion of beingless objects. Consider, for example, Quine's 'virtual classes'.[14] Virtual classes are virtually like other classes except that they do not exist. Why are they important? Because it is by means of them that Quine endeavors to ascertain just where assumptions of existence intrude in the corpus of set theory and its progeny – number theory, for example. Quine, of course, regards talk of virtual classes qua things merely as ways of speaking, devoid of any ontic commitment. In his development they are introduced into the theory by way of those sleight-of-hand devices called contextual definitions; they enter and depart from calculations only verbally. But there is a development of virtual classes, explored by Dana Scott,[15] in which they are treated more 'substantially'; here virtual class names name things, and beingless things at that. What is especially important for the present concern is Scott's discovery that to treat virtual classes as entities is simpler and more elegant than Quine's

[13] See also the second edition (Barth, Leipzig, 1910), where there are important addenda about objectives.
[14] W. V. Quine, *Set Theory and its Logic*, Harvard University Press, Cambridge, Mass., 1969.
[15] Dana Scott, 'Existence and Description in Formal Logic' in R. Schoenman (ed.), *Bertrand Russell: Philosopher of the Century*, Allen and Unwin, London, 1967.

façon de parler treatment.[16] So there is apparently a definite theoretical advantage in admitting those beingless objects called virtual classes – a kind of theoretical advantage, that of simplicity, which Quine himself thoroughly embraces.

Talk of beingless objects leads sooner or later to that philosophical doctrine associated with the famous names of Hegel, Bradley and Bosanquet: *absolute idealism*. If we consider Bradley, for him the objects of sight no more exist than does the passage of the earth around the sun, despite what one actually sees virtually every morning – at least in the smogless parts of southern California. Nor is this position, in Parsons' words, 'metaphysically boring';[17] the objects which have being are mental, not physical. In short, for Bradley there are objects that do not exist.

The case of Bradley's version of absolute idealism is noteworthy for two main reasons. First, apparently without the conception of beingless object – or at least nonexistent object – his doctrine cannot even be stated, let alone assessed for truth-value. Second, the evanescent and fuzzy nature of many allegedly beingless objects – and the attendant worry about their identity conditions in the minds of many – is contravened in the case of some of Bradley's candidates. For no one has similar concerns about physical objects, a category that doesn't exist (and may not have being either) for Bradley.

A fourth, and by no means the last, Meinongian idea of considerable importance for contemporary analytic philosophy is his principle of the independence of being and being so, which is the major topic of this book. This principle, loosely speaking a principle about objects and properties, has important semantic consequences. The most common rendition of the principle in fact is that an object, though beingless (hence nonexistent), can have properties. Meinong himself used as examples (confirming the principle) the beingless objects the gold mountain and the round square:

---

[16] Dana Scott, 'Advice on Modal Logic', in Karel Lambert (ed.), *Philosophical Problems in Logic* (Reidel, Dordrecht, 1969), p. 146.

[17] *Nonexistent Objects*, p. 230.

The area of applicability of this principle is best illustrated by consideration of the following circumstance: the principle applies, not only to Objects which do not exist in fact, but also to Objects which could not exist because they are impossible. Not only is the much heralded gold mountain made of gold, but the round square is as surely round as it is square.[18]

An important consequence of the principle of independence, via semantic ascent, is that a statement, perhaps simple, containing a singular term '*t*', can be true though the statement that *t* subsists (has being) is false. For example, borrowing from the previous quotation, a Meinongian would cite as confirmatory evidence the truth of the statement 'The round square is a round square' and the falsity of the statement 'The round square subsists (has being)'.

One reason why Meinong's principle of independence and its semantic reflection are important is that, to put it paradoxically, one can accept the pair of them without being Meinongian. What I mean is that the principle of independence does not by itself imply that there are nonsubsistent objects. The reason for this will emerge in the next two chapters. Yet it is the most distinctive principle in the Meinongian world picture, another point which finds support in the next chapter. But its importance transcends its exact position in Meinong's theory of objects. In particular, there are certain versions of free logic – a species of logic admitting singular terms that do not refer to existents – which conform to the principle of independence. It is a principle bearing directly on the theory of predication, and a principle rejected by Frege and Russell, and even by many free logicians – in other words, virtually by the mainstream in contemporary philosophical logic – and espoused only by a radical few. Arguments, therefore, directly or indirectly for the principle of independence are both reasons against the mainstream treatment of predication in philosophical logic and reasons in favor of a particular formulation out of the plethora of versions of free logic. It is a

[18] 'On the Theory of Objects', p. 82.

concern that should be of more than passing interest to contemporary philosophers of language and logic, as later chapters will, I hope, confirm.

It is not difficult, then, to cite features of Meinong's thought which are of interest and relevance to current analytic philosophy. These examples, easy to multiply, give the lie to an all-too-common picture of Meinong's historical position shared even by many of those who do not regard Meinong as philosophically inept. That picture emerges clearly in a well-intentioned passage from a sympathetic essay commemorating Meinong's thought by that justly esteemed analytic philosopher, Gilbert Ryle. Ryle writes:

first let us acknowledge it as a perfectly general truth, a truth of which Hegel was well aware, that philosophy is always indebted to its original thinkers, Russell as well as Meinong, Kant as well as Hume, Aristotle as well as Plato, not only for the forward steps that each of them took, but also for those forward steps that each by his 'thus far and no farther' provoked his successors into taking. In the game of leapfrog the place where one player stops is just the place from which his successor vaults ahead. So, though no thinker could relish the idea that he too was soon to be overtaken and then left behind, each thinker knows well that he owes the very possibility of his own finest advances to those predecessors who had stopped just short of making them. The Pioneer's new track round the swamp brings all his successors right up to the thicket that he had not even seen. Russell and Wittgenstein needed to have Meinong to vault over...[19]

There is an unmistakable tone in this passage that Meinong is out of date. It suggests that after Russell and Wittgenstein, Meinong's ideas took on the character of archaeological relics, to be admired in philosophical museums, but certainly not items that any current analytic philosopher could expect to find useful. This view of the usefulness of Meinong's thought is not only wrong in detail but is conditioned by an inadequate

---

[19] G. Ryle, 'Intentionality: Theory and the Nature of Thinking', in R. Haller (ed.), *Jenseits von Sein und Nichtsein* (Akademische Druck-u. Verlagsanstalt, Graz, 1972), pp. 8–9.

view of progress in philosophy. The leapfrog image certainly is not always appropriate; philosophical progress is sometimes more like the childhood game of giant-step – a step forward sometimes requires two steps back to understand how to avoid unanticipated dead ends occasioned by that initial, and presumed to be progressive, step. Contemporary philosophical logic affords, for example, culs-de-sac aplenty for the Russellian theory of nominative expressions; therefore a sensible procedure is to reexamine the path Meinong and others such as Brentano blazed 'around the swamp'. I hope that the rest of this work will help to motivate others to travel Meinong's original though now much overgrown path, and perhaps to discover potential routes through the thicket that more athletic and impatient philosophers were fated to miss.

BEING AND INDEPENDENCE

I. OBJECTS AND THE PRINCIPLE OF INDEPENDENCE

Meinong said that

the totality of what exists, including what has existed and will exist, is infinitely small in comparison with the totality of the objects of knowledge. This fact easily goes unnoticed, probably because the lively interest in reality which is part of our nature tends to favor that exaggeration which finds the non-real a mere nothing... or, more precisely, which finds the non-real to be something for which science has no application or at least no application of any worth.[1]

Indeed, he believed the attitude expressed in the final sentence of this passage to be quite unjustified. Take the case of mathematical objects – the number 2 or the set of astronauts, for example. No one denies, he would have said, that they are objects of considerable scientific interest even though they do not exist. Reflecting the Humean influence of his early philosophical training under Brentano, Meinong held that *existent* objects are objects having location in space-time; objects not spatio-temporally locatable but nevertheless having being he called (merely) *subsistent* objects. And among the latter are all sorts of interesting entities: not only the vast array of mathematical objects, but also, for instance, ideal relations such as similarity, and many of the proposition-like entities he called objectives. The difference between (merely) subsistent objects and existent objects corresponds very roughly to the currently

---

[1] Meinong, 'On The Theory of Objects'. This essay is an English translation by I. Levi, D. B. Terrell and R. M. Chisholm of Meinong's 'Über Gegenstandstheorie'. It first appeared in a collection of essays by Meinong and his associates, entitled *Untersuchungen zur Gegenstandstheorie und Psychologie* and edited by Meinong (Barth, Leipzig, 1904).

popular distinction between abstract and concrete objects.[2]

What really sets Meinong apart from the majority of philosophers, however, is not the distinction between the two kinds of being an object might possess[3] – a view, after all, advocated in one form or another by many philosophers from Aristotle on; rather, it is his belief in *nonsubsistent* objects, objects that have neither existence or subsistence (nor any other kind of being), that is truly distinctive. From time to time, and especially in unpublished lectures toward the end of his career, Meinong did toy with the idea of a pervasive kind of being possessed by all objects.[4] But most Meinong scholars agree that Meinong's most widely promulgated (and most interesting) insight is that there are objects having no being in some appropriate sense of 'there are'.[5] Certainly this is the position in 'Über Gegenstandstheorie', the most explicit statement of his considered thought. Those having a taste for paradoxical ways of speaking, he said, would appreciate another statement of the position: There are objects such that there are no such objects.[6]

The domain of nonbeings Meinong called '*Aussersein*', literally the domain of objects outside of being.[7] Among the denizens of *Aussersein* are possible objects such as Pegasus and

---

[2] See, for example, H. S. Leonard, *Principles of Reasoning,* Dover, New York, 1967, for a discussion of this distinction, and also Quine, *Methods of Logic* (revised edn), Holt-Dryden, New York, 1959.

[3] He seems to have believed that the existent objects formed a proper subset of the subsistent objects, which in turn formed a proper subset of the objects in general. For authoritative support of this interpretation of Meinong's views on existence and subsistence see N. Findlay's splendid book *Meinong's Theory of Objects and Values*, p. 114, n. 1. See also Meinong's 'Über Gegenstandstheorie', p. 39; 'Über Annahmen', p. 14; and 'Selbstdarstellung', p. 18, in *Gesamtausgabe* (ed. R. Haller and R. Kindinger), Akademische Druck-u. Verlagsanstalt, Graz, 1969–78.

[4] Two of these unpublished manuscripts are his lectures entitled 'Gegenstandstheoretische Logik' (1913) and 'Wahrheit und Wahrscheinlichkeit' (1915). These can be found among Meinong's collected writings in the library of the Karl Franzens Universität in Graz, Austria. I am especially indebted to Dr Raeinhard Fabian for digging up these sources of Meinong's later thought.

[5] See, for example, J. N. Findlay's comments in the second edition of *Meinong's Theory of Objects and Values*, pp. 46–7, and R. M. Chisholm's presentation of Meinong's views in his essay 'Beyond Being and Nonbeing' in *Jenseits von Sein und Nichtsein*, pp. 25–6.

[6] 'On the Theory of Objects', p. 83.

[7] Meinong's notion of being corresponds fairly closely to Quine's broad and univocal sense of 'existence.' The proper philosophical adversary of Quine's theory of exist-

the golden mountain, and impossible objects such as the round square of Mill and the proof of the decidability of general quantification theory. So, contrary to a wide misunderstanding of Meinong, the world of nonbeings does not consist just of the (merely) possible objects.[8]

What was the foundation of Meinong's belief in *Aussersein*? One reason, essentially a negative one, concerns the relationship between what he called objectives and their constituents. In the third chapter of *Über Annahmen*, Meinong introduces the notion of objective (*Objektiv*) in the following way:

> If someone says, e.g., in regard to a parliamentary election, that was preceded by intense public excitement, that no disturbance of the peace took place, then in the first place no one will deny that 'something' is known by means of the judgment in question – assuming that it is quite correct... As soon as one attempts to give a closer account of this 'something', it becomes evident that under ordinary conditions, if we want to avoid artificial constructions, a single word is not readily at our disposal for this purpose; yet a sentence with 'that' offers itself as an entirely natural means of expression. In the case of our example, what I know is simply 'that no disturbances of the peace have occurred'... There arises the need to extend the sense of the term 'object of judgment', at least enough to include objects of the type just considered. Yet there is also a need to give these latter objects a special name in order to distinguish them from what was formerly looked on as the sole object of judgment, i.e., the object that representation presents to judgment for a sort of working over – that is, the representational object. It seemed most appropriate for me to use the name 'objectives' for the new class of judgmental objects characterized by the above remarks.[9]

---

ence, then, is Meinong; whereas the former abhors nonexistents, in the broad sense of 'exists', the latter embraces them.

[8] It would be a mistake, therefore, to identify the interpretation of many inner domain–outer domain semantics for free logic as Meinongian – for example, Dana Scott's recent version; see his 'Advice on Modal Logic'. Scott's innermost domain consists of the existents. It is a subset of the outer domain of possible objects. (There is also an outermost 'domain' of virtual 'objects' but no quantifier of any kind ranges over the 'objects' in it. Hence the scare quotes around 'domain' and 'object'. Meinong, in contrast, requires quantification over all kinds of nonexistent objects.)

[9] *On Assumptions* (English translation of *Über Annahmen* by James Hearne; University of California Press, forthcoming).

So, an objective is the kind of object referred to by a that-clause or meant by the statement suffixed to 'that' in the that-clause. The objective that Oslo is in Norway, for example, is referred to by 'that Oslo is in Norway' and is meant by 'Oslo is in Norway.'

Objectives differ from the other major class of objects, objecta (*Objekta*), because the latter can be constituents of the former but not vice versa. Thus 'Oslo' names an object which is a constituent of the objective that Oslo is in Norway, but that objective, though capable of constituency in yet further, more complex objectives, can never be a constituent of an object such as Oslo. Like propositions, objectives can be true or false, but unlike propositions they are not *made* true or false by anything, viz., the facts. Objectives, like objecta, can have being, but unlike objecta they cannot have existence (for example, the objective that Oslo is in Norway or the objective that the round square is round). Also they can have nonbeing (for example, the objective that Oslo is in Sweden or the objective that the round square is possible). Objectives that have being are said to possess factuality – or, more idiomatically, *are* facts.

In 'On the Theory of Objects' Meinong rejects the conviction that the constituents of objectives must have being if the objectives containing them do. It is based, he believes, on a 'questionable analogy' with the part–whole relation. He says:

this requirement is based solely on the analogy to the part–whole relation: an Objective is thereby treated as a complex of some kind and the Object belonging to it as a kind of component. In many respects this may be in accordance with our insight into the nature of an Objective, which is as yet still exceedingly defective. However, no one will deny that this analogy is only an initial expedient in our embarrassment and that there would be no grounds for following this analogy rigorously even for part of the way. Thus, instead of deriving the being of an Object from the being of an Objective, even on the basis of a questionable analogy where the Objective is an Objective of non-being, it would be better to conclude from the facts with which we are concerned that this analogy does not apply to the Objective of non-being – i.e., that the being of the Objective is not by any means universally dependent upon the being of its Object.[10]

So the relationship between objective and constituent is not like the part–whole relation at all, and the major reason for believing that the constituents of factual objectives must have being collapses.

The positive reason for Meinong's belief in *Aussersein* is metaphysical: *what* an object is is a function solely of its *nature*. It is in virtue of their natures that camels have humps, the number one is prime, and Mill's round square is round. That an object is what it is need not depend on, or even concern, its being.

On the face of it common sense favors this metaphysical position. To see this one need only imagine a youngster excitedly reporting to a friend who Marie Antoinette was, or what the guillotine is, having just collected this information in one of the more gory of his usually boring history classes. The being of the haughty queen or of the dreaded instrument of execution need not, and probably never does, arise. Similarly, one can imagine our young reporter on another occasion regaling the same friend with an account of who Sherlock Holmes is, or what the League of Red-Haired Men was, having just gleaned this important information in an English literature class. Certainly the existence or being of these objects does not appear to be vital to the who or the what of the objects portrayed by the young narrator.

Of course, these examples are not compelling evidence against the being of fictional objects, in some sense of 'being'. Although they seem to indicate that fictional objects can have characteristics without having existence, or subsistence, they do not establish that they have characteristics without having some kind of being, since the examples are consistent with the view that all fictional objects (and perhaps all objects) have some kind of being. They are at best what in the Middle Ages were called 'inclining reasons' for the nonbeing of Holmes and

---

[10] 'On the Theory of Objects', pp. 84–5.

the League. Some of Meinong's more substantial reasons for the beinglessness of fictional objects will be discussed briefly in the last section of this chapter.

The positive reason for Meinong's belief in beingless objects leads directly into the major topic of concern of this book – the principle of the independence of nature (*Sosein*) from being (*Sein*). This principle, hereinafter called simply the principle of independence, was borrowed by Meinong from his student Ernst Mally,[11] and is surely the most distinctive principle in his unconventional if common-sense theory of objects. Though Meinong's initial discussion and defense of the principle in 'On the Theory of Objects' concerns the narrower notion of existence,[12] clearly he envisages the principle as extending to the wider notion of being,[13] an extension on which the discussion here relies. Even so, the principle stands in need of clarification; for example, Meinong's conception of the nature of an object needs to be unraveled, as does the force of the metaphysical buzz-word 'independent'.

II. ON THE NATURES OF OBJECTS

What constitutes the nature of an object? The answer is: *all* the object's *nuclear properties*. The best place to begin an exploration of this answer is with an explanation of the difference between the principle of independence and another principle which Meinong dubs 'the principle of the indifference of the pure object to being' – hereinafter simply *'the principle of indifference'*.

Concerning the principle of indifference, Meinong writes that

neither being nor non-being can belong essentially to the Object in

---

[11] 'On the Theory of Objects', p. 82; see especially n. 7. In later years Mally rejected the principle.

[12] *Ibid.* Here Meinong appeals to the consideration that merely subsistent geometrical entities have properties though they do not exist; for example, triangles though nonexistent are bounded figures.

[13] *Ibid.*, pp. 83–8. For authoritative support, see also Chisholm's remark on Mally's statement in the first paragraph of his essay, 'Beyond Being and Nonbeing', p. 25.

itself. This is not to say, of course, that an Object can neither be nor not be. Nor is it to say that the question, whether or not the Object has being, is purely accidental to the nature of every Object. An absurd Object such as a round square carries in itself the guarantee of its own non-being in every sense; an ideal Object, such as diversity, carries in itself the guarantee of its own non-existence. Anyone who seeks to associate himself with models which have become famous could formulate what has been shown above by saying that the Object as such (without considering the occasional peculiarities or the accompanying Objective-clause which is always present) stands 'beyond being and non-being'. This may also be expressed in the following less engaging and also less pretentious way, which is in my opinion, however, a more appropriate one: The Object is by nature indifferent to being (*ausserseiend*), although at least one of its two Objectives of being, the Object's being or non-being, subsists.[14]

The principle of indifference declares that the being or nonbeing of an object is not part of the nature of that object; that is, to paraphrase Findlay, whether objects are or are not makes no difference to what they are.[15] Though the principle of indifference is often run together with the principle of independence, there is no doubt that Meinong himself considered them to be distinct, as is evident in the following remark: 'the

[14] *Ibid.*, p. 86.
[15] *Meinong's Theory of Objects and Values*, p. 75. In his interesting essay, 'Meinongian Theories and a Russellian Paradox', *Noûs* 12, (1978), William Rapaport holds that neither being nor nonbeing is 'properly predicable of objecta' but rather that both are 'properly predicable only of objectives'. It is in this way, he says, that one can see 'there is some sense in saying' that the pure object stands beyond being and nonbeing (p. 157). I find this interpretation of Meinong's remarks in 'On the Theory of Objects' strained. In the first place, it isn't clear what Rapaport means by 'properly predicable' because he also speaks of *ascribing* '*Sein*' to an objective'. In the second place, I don't think Meinong's metaphor that the pure object is beyond being and nonbeing particularly mysterious, or requires the interpretation Rapaport puts on Meinong's remarks to prevent incoherence. On the contrary, it seems quite clear what Meinong means by that metaphor in his famous discussion of the principle of indifference in 'On the Theory of Objects' (p. 86); he means that 'neither being nor nonbeing can belong essentially to the object in itself'. In the third place, Meinong speaks of the principle of independence as a 'supplement' to the principle of indifference, that from the pair of them one can infer 'that that which is not in any way external to the object, but constitutes its proper essence, subsists in its *Sosein*'. But how one could infer this, given that being and nonbeing are properly only properties of objectives, while the principle of independence is taken to be about a certain relation between an object's nature and *its* nonbeing, would truly be mysterious.

above mentioned principle of the independence of *Sosein* from *Sein* now presents a welcome supplement to the principle that the subject is by nature indifferent to being.'[16]

How then are these two principles to be distinguished? The answer is that the principle of indifference says something about the makeup of the nature of the object, but the principle of independence does not. This is an important answer because despite its tone the principle of indifference is not peculiarly characteristic of the Meinongian world picture. A more conventional philosopher – Kant, for instance, who, according to many, subscribed to the view that every object has being – could feel quite comfortable with the principle of indifference. As Findlay puts it, 'the fact of existence seems wholly alien and extrinsic [to what the object is], which is the point stressed by Kant when he maintained that existence was not a genuine predicate of things'.[17]

The principle of independence, however, licenses the maxim that an object's nature, whatever its makeup, attaches to it even if it has no being, and indeed peculiarly characterizes the Meinongian world picture, if any single principle does. At one place Meinong expresses the principle of independence this way:

the *Sosein* of an Object is not affected by its *Nichtsein*. The fact is sufficiently important to be explicitly formulated as the principle of the independence of *Sosein* from *Sein*. The area of applicability of this principle is best illustrated by consideration of the following circumstance: the principle applies, not only to Objects which do not exist in fact, but also to Objects which could not exist because they are impossible. Not only is the much heralded gold mountain made of gold, but the round square is as surely round as it is square.[18]

Though the principle of indifference demands that the nature of the round square, for example, not include its nonbeing, this does not mean, Meinong holds, that the nature

---

[16] 'On the Theory of Objects', p. 86.
[17] *Meinong's Theory of Objects and Values*, p. 49. It is clear from the context that 'being' can be substituted for 'existence' in the passage cited.
[18] 'On the Theory of Objects', p. 82.

of the round square does not 'guarantee its nonbeing'.[19] In other words, the nonbeing of an object may be guaranteed by its nature, yet the object by nature can still be indifferent to being; that the nonbeing of the round square, for example, is *guaranteed* by its nature does not mean that the nonbeing of that object is *part* of its nature. In the logician's idiom, given that the nature of an object is a set of properties and the relation *part of* is *membership*, natures are not closed under guarantees.

The discussion so far has fixed on what is *not* in the nature of an object; in particular, being and nonbeing are not parts of the natures of objects.[20] Let us continue in the same vein for a

---

[19] In an earlier essay, one which formed the basis of this chapter, I observed that the objective that $2 + 2 = 4$ guaranteed its factuality. That remark was based on the suggestion that 'factuality' – the synonym of 'being' where talk about objectives is concerned – though 'more intimately' related to objectives than being is to objecta, still is not part of the nature of objectives. But I now have doubts about that inference. For one thing it is difficult to find any direct textual evidence supporting the inference. This has an effect on the current interpretation of the principle of independence as the reader may observe by comparing the earlier essay with this chapter. See Karel Lambert, 'A Logical Reconstruction of Meinong's Principle of Independence', *Topoi*, forthcoming.

[20] Chisholm and Findlay hold that Meinong's view is that being and nonbeing are not properties of objecta. (For Chisholm's statement see *Realism and the Background of Phenomenology*, p. 10, and for Findlay's position see *Meinong's Theory of Objects and Values*, p. 103.) But there lingers the suspicion that Meinong, in fact, did not deny the status of property to being and nonbeing as applied to objecta. (In the case of objectives being (factuality) and nonbeing (unfactuality) unquestionably *are* properties.) First, much of the discussion of being and nonbeing in the first four sections of 'The Theory of Objects' is couched in terms such as 'ascribe', 'belong', etc., strongly suggesting that being and nonbeing are properties. Second, even some of the authorities backslide on the matter. For example, Findlay speaks of Meinong 'attributing some sort of being' to fictional objects in the doctrine of pseudo-existence (see *Meinong's Theory of Objects and Values*, 2nd edn, p. 21). Third, other students of Meinong's theory of objects interpret being to be a property even when applied to objecta, *contra* Chisholm and Findlay (see, for example, Rapaport, 'Meinongian Theories and a Russellian Paradox', p. 157). Fourth, consider Chisholm's account of *Sosein* (nature). For Chisholm it is a set of characteristics or properties. But if being (and nonbeing) are not properties, then it would be trivial that the object is by nature indifferent to being. Yet the involved discussion surrounding this principle in 'The Theory of Objects' belies this construal; no such reason for the principle of indifference is even hinted at by Meinong. Finally, 'being' and 'nonbeing' seem to belong to a class of descriptions, the other members of which are said to denote 'extranuclear' properties, properties 'founded' on, but not part of, the natures of objecta. Another example is the word 'possibility'. Why 'being' and 'nonbeing' should be treated so differently is puzzling, nor is it easy to find evidence that Meinong in fact does so treat them.

moment. What else is excluded from the nature of an object?[21]
Examples are simplicity, possibility, and determinateness.
Why are such properties excluded from the nature of objects?
As one might expect, different properties require different
reasons. But an example may be helpful. Consider the
property of simplicity. Meinong recognized the existence of
simple particulars, that is, particulars having a nature consisting of exactly one property. For example, a certain shade of
blue is a simple particular; so, for Meinong, it would be true to
say 'This shade of blue is simple.' But if simplicity were part of
the nature of this shade of blue, it would contain at least the
two properties, being blue and being simple, and thus would
turn a simple object into a complex one. Simplicity, therefore,
cannot be a part of the nature of this shade of blue. In general,
were simplicity part of the natures of simple objects, there
could be only one simple.[22] Such properties of objects, then,
though 'founded' on what these objects are, are not part of
what they are. On the other hand, properties like being black-
haired, being courageous, or being even are properties of
objects that constitute parts of their natures. These properties
Meinong called nuclear (*konstitutorische*) properties, and the
former kind he called extranuclear (*ausserkonstitutorische*)
properties. Meinong himself puts the distinction this way: 'for
the collection of constitutive and consecutive determinators
[of an object] I propose the name "nuclear", and for the
remaining determinations, the name "extranuclear".[23]

It was Meinong's view that if a property is possessed by an
object and if it is not extranuclear, then it is part of the nature
of the object.[24] Thus one arrives at his view that the nature of

---

[21] The rest of this discussion about natures is by and large in terms of objecta.

[22] This presumes, of course, that object *a* is the same as object *b* just in case what they
are is the same – that is, that every nuclear property *a* has *b* has.

[23] *Möglichkeit und Wahrscheinlichkeit* (revised by R. Chisholm, Akademische Druck-u.
Verlagsanstalt, Graz, 1972), p. 176; my translation. See also Terence Parsons,
'Nuclear and Extranuclear Properties, Meinong and Leibniz', *Noûs* 12 (1978), pp.
137–53, for an interesting reconstruction of the Mally–Meinong notion of *ausserkonstitutorische Eigenschaften*.

[24] 'On the Theory of Objects', p. 86.

an object is all and only its nuclear properties.[25]

III. ON THE LOGICAL NATURE OF INDEPENDENCE

The word 'independent', like the word 'prior' in 'Essence is prior to being', though intended to express an important and profound relationship, is seldom very clearly explained by metaphysicians, and Meinong is no exception. Usually what is meant is some kind of logical relationship, and in the case of the Mally–Meinong principle under examination the suggestion is overwhelming.

Three passages, one from Meinong's essay 'On the Theory of Objects', and the others from Mally's essay 'On the Object Theory of Measurement', will dramatize the point. Thus Meinong says:

Now it would accord very well with the aforementioned prejudice in favor of existence to hold that we may speak of a *Sosein* only if a *Sein* is presupposed. There would, indeed, be little sense in calling a house large or small, a region fertile or unfertile, before one knew that the house or the land does exist, has existed, or will exist. However, the very science from which we were able to obtain the largest number of instances counter to this prejudice shows clearly that any such principle is untenable. As we know, the figures with which geometry is concerned do not exist. Nevertheless, their properties, and hence their *Sosein*, can be established. Doubtless, in the area of what can be known merely *a posteriori*, a claim as to *Sosein* will be completely unjustifiable if it is not based on knowledge of a *Sein*; it is equally certain that a *Sosein* which does not rest on a *Sein* may often enough be utterly lacking in natural interest. None of this alters the fact that the *Sosein* of an Object is not affected by its *Nichtsein*.[26]

Mally introduces the principle of independence this way:

Every object either is or is not. Nevertheless every object is constitu-

---

[25] I have not been concerned here to challenge Meinong's positions and distinctions, only to explain them. Of course, as I will argue later, there is considerable plausibility to Meinong's principle of independence – or at least to a liberalized reconstruction of that principle – despite the worth, or lack of worth, of his own reasons for promoting this principle.

[26] *Ibid.*, p. 82.

ted in some way. So every object, whether having being or not having being, has properties (*Sosein*). An object's having properties is independent of its being (*Sein*). An all-knowing man, for example, is all-knowing even if he does not exist...[27]

A little later he comments on the 'converse' relation of being and having properties:

The relation of independence between having properties (*Sosein*) and being (*Sein*) is not properly convertible (*umkehrbar*): the being of an object is not independent of the properties it has. To show this it is enough to note the fact that something cannot be because it has properties which exclude its being. This is the case for each object with contradictory properties. The 'round square' is not because it is round and square.[28]

Thus, in his discussion of the principle in 'On the Theory of Objects', Meinong says that though one's interest in what characteristics a thing has or does not have may rest on one's presumption that the thing has being, it is not the case that an object's having characteristics presupposes its being, that having a nature presupposes that it *is*.[29] The two occurrences of the word 'presupposes' suggest strongly a certain semantical relationship receiving diverse treatments in the philosophical logic of the last two decades.[30] In Mally's discussion, words like 'excludes' and phrases such as 'properly convertible' support the suggestion that 'independence' expresses a logical relationship of some kind.

How then is the relationship expressed by 'The nature (*Sosein*) of an object is independent of the being (*Sein*) of that object' to be understood? Beginning where intentions are most clearly expressed, consider Mally's assertion that being (*Sein*) is not independent of nature – or more literally, that being is

[27] E. Mally, 'Zur Gegenstandstheorie des Messens' (On the Object Theory of Measurement), in A. Meinong (ed.), *Untersuchungen zur Gegenstandstheorie und Psychologie* (Barth, Leipzig, 1904), p. 126; my translation.

[28] *Ibid.*, p. 127; my translation.

[29] 'On the Theory of Objects', p. 82.

[30] See for example, Bas van Fraassen, 'Presupposition, Supervaluations and Free Logic', in Karel Lambert (ed.), *The Logical Way of Doing Things*, Yale University Press, New Haven, 1969; and also the paper by Nuel Belnap in the same volume.

not independent of the having of properties (*Sosein*). Adapting the results of the discussion in the previous section, Mally's dictum can be put as follows: it is logically true that there are nuclear properties P_1, P_2 ... such that if the set of nuclear properties P_1, P_2 ... attaches to s then s does not have being.[31] This, in turn, is equivalent to: it is logically true that if s has being then there are nuclear properties P_1, P_2 ... such that it is not the case that the set of nuclear properties P_1, P_2 ... attaches to s. More perspicuously, the last statement says: the statement that s has being *logically implies* the statement that there are nuclear properties P_1, P_2 ... such that it is not the case that the set of nuclear properties P_1, P_2 ... attaches to s. Recast into Mally's language this last statement is the principle that being excludes some natures – or, more literally, that being excludes the having of some (nuclear) properties. This, in fact, is quite harmonious with Mally's remarks in the second of the passages quoted above.

A very important principle in the Meinongian theory of

[31] The word 'attaches' is Meinong's expression for the relation between nature (*Sosein*) and object. See 'On the Theory of Objects', p. 86. The expressions 'P_1', 'P_2' are variables ranging over properties – for instance, being Austrian, preferring objects, subsistent, and so on. The expression 's' is a variable ranging over objects – for instance, Meinong, the round square, that Oslo is in Norway, and so on.

In this treatise statements (and statement forms) receive the preferential nod over objectives (and objective forms) in talk about the principle of independence. (In fact, Chisholm's own defense of the doctrine of *Aussersein* in 'Beyond Being and Nonbeing' appeals to statements rather than objectives; see pp. 25–33.) For it is not at all clear that even objectives, let alone objective forms, are legitimate terms to any relation of independence because their status as the bearers of truth and falsehood, properties in terms of which implication (and independence) are defined, is very unclear. Findlay reports that, strictly speaking, truth (and falsehood) are not properties of an objective, that though it may be natural to regard truth-values as properties of objectives, they may indeed with propriety be thought of as properties of the 'apprehended objective', of a judgment, a surmise, a belief, a supposition, and so on. No doubt part of the reason for this 'subjective' view of truth is that objectives can also be facts and facts normally are thought to be the sort of thing that *makes* whatever is true (or false), true (or false) not as that sort of thing which is true (or false); see *Meinong's Theory of Objects and Values*, esp. pp. 84–9 and pp. 186–7. Finally, I am well aware that explicating Meinong's relation of independence as independence of statement forms saddles him via their instances, with an unrelativized truth-value vehicle – statements – which upon reflection he may have wished to reject. However, in my opinion this would require a very different exposition of that principle than he gives in 'On the Theory of Objects'. The present 'reconstruction' of the principle of independence, I think, is quite faithful to Meinong's intentions there.

objects is that if an object has being, it is completely determined.[32] In the context of the present discussion this principle
may be represented as follows: it is logically true that for any
property P, if s has being, then if P is not among the set of
properties attaching to s, then the complement of P (non-P) is
among the set of properties attaching to s.[33] By virtue of this
principle, the Meinong–Mally principle that being excludes
the having of some (nuclear) properties yields the principle
that being includes the having of some (nuclear) properties
(namely, the complements of those (nuclear) properties
excluded by it). In fact, the two principles are logically equivalent. Formally represented, the inclusion principle looks like
this: the statement that s has being logically implies the statement that there are nuclear properties P_1, P_2 ... such that the
set of nuclear properties P_1, P_2 attaches to s.

[32] Authoritative support for this claim is most easily found in Findlay. See *Meinong's
Theory of Objects and Values*, p. 156.

[33] All objects having being are, for Meinong, *complete* objects. He also distinguished a
class of objects called *incomplete* objects. Though they play little part in this book, a
few words about them are in order here.
   An incomplete object is one such that for some property P – presumably a nuclear
one – the object neither has nor lacks P; in other words, it neither possesses P nor
possesses non-P. Meinong explains and illustrates his doctrine with the help of the
incomplete object 'blue (as such)' in *Über Möglichkeit und Wahrscheinlichkeit* (On
Possibility and Probability) (revised by R. M. Chisholm; Akademische Druck-u.
Verlaganstalt, Graz, 1972). On p. 171 he says:

> it is inappropriate to say blue (as such) is extended or unextended as it is to say,
> contrarily, that extension is blue or nonblue. If an object A is, then, called deter-
> mined with respect to an object B, when one can correctly assert of A that it is B or
> that it is not B, blue (as such) is undetermined with respect to extension, and
> further the law of the excluded third ... can no longer be legitimately applied to
> blue in abstraction.

Incomplete objects are more like Platonic forms than Fregeian senses. Yet even
though the chair as such qua incomplete object *is* a chair, it is used by Meinong as
an intermediary in reference by a person to a complete object. In 'I saw a man' reference is made to a complete object – a definite man, as Russell would say – by way of
the perceived incomplete object man (as such). Another important use of incomplete objects is in an alternative account of the bearers of modal properties. It makes
no sense, Meinong believed, to say the actual desk (on which I am writing) might be
blue if it is in fact brown. What we are really talking about, when we say things such
as 'The desk might be blue', is rather the desk as such – an incomplete object. For
further discussion of this radical view see R. M. Chisholm's essay 'Homeless
Objects', *Revue Internationale de Philosophie*, 104–5 (1973). Finally, it ought at least to
be mentioned that incomplete objects play a major role in Terence Parsons' recent
Meinong-motivated theory of beingless objects; see his *Nonexistent Objects*.

What has been explicated by means of the notion of logical implication has been Mally's assertion that the 'converse' of the principle of independence of *Sosein* from *Sein* does not hold: *Sein* is not independent from *Sosein*, he says. What has also been shown is that the principle so explicated is logically equivalent to the principle that *Sein* includes *Sosein*.

Turning now to the principle of independence itself, extrapolation from Meinong's and Mally's remarks and examples suggests that Mally and Meinong are denying that nonbeing excludes the having of properties. Recall, for example, Meinong's remark that the *Sosein* of an object is not affected by its *Nichtsein* (nonbeing). In other words, they are rejecting the logical implication from the statement that s does not have being to the statement that there are no nuclear properties P_1, P_2 ... such that the set of nuclear properties P_1, P_2 ... attaches to s. Two questions of importance are: What does this explication amount to? and, Is the rejected implication the logical converse of the implication explicating the nonindependence of *Sein* from *Sosein*? An affirmative answer to the latter question will bolster the suspicion expressed above that the Meinong–Mally conception of independence is a logical notion.

Concerning the first of these questions, help is provided by an analogue of the logical notion of contraposition. The 'contrapositive' of the statement 'A logically implies B' is the statement 'not B logically implies not A'. When a statement of the first form is true, so is the second, and vice versa. Now the 'contrapositive' of the logical implication being rejected by Meinong and Mally is this: the statement that there are nuclear properties P_1, P_2 ... such that the set of nuclear properties P_1, P_2 ... attaches to s logically implies the statement that s has being. *Eureka!* Notice, first, that the implication just stated (which is equivalent to that rejected by Meinong and Mally) *is* the logical converse of that explicating the principle that *Sein* includes *Sosein*. And this in turn we have seen, is equivalent to the nonindependence of *Sein* from *Sosein*. Notice, second, that if the independence of *Sosein* from *Sein* is explicated as the *rejection* introduced early in the previous paragraph, then indeed its 'converse' *does* fail. So there is clear support for the idea that the Meinong–Mally notion of nonindependence is captured with the help of the notion of logical implication.

Another benefit of dwelling on the 'contrapositive' is this: rejection of the logical implication so revealed is a particularly perspicuous way of understanding what Meinong and Mally had in mind. For it amounts to saying that the inference from the statement 'there are nuclear properties $P_1, P_2 \ldots$ such that the set of nuclear properties attaches to s' to the statement 's has being' is invalid. More will be made of this point shortly, but let me note now that it is the version of the principle of independence which forms the basis for all subsequent discussion: that is, the principle of independence, in what I shall call the strict sense, is henceforth the claim that the argument

There are nuclear properties $P_1, P_2 \ldots$ such that the set of $P_1, P_2 \ldots$ attaches to s;
So, s has being

is invalid.

An important suppressed principle in Meinong's theory of objects is that if a property Q is a member of s's nature, then Q is possessed by s – that is, $Q\, s$. Indeed, Meinong suggests a stronger principle in 'On the Theory of Objects', namely, that if Q is not an extranuclear property, then Q is a member of the nature of s, *if and only if* Q is possessed by s.[34] The main reason the principle mentioned at the beginning of this paragraph is important is because presumably it is what is behind the more common version of the Meinong-Mally principle of independence one sees in the authorities. Mention of a relation of attachment between nature and object seldom occurs; rather, the principle usually gets expressed as the maxim that an

---

[34] 'On the Theory of Objects', p. 86. It is this principle, no doubt, that underlies the observation, discussed in the previous section, that for Meinong the nature of an object consists of all its nuclear properties, both those traditionally called 'essential' and those traditionally called 'accidental'. How Meinong is nevertheless able to maintain a version of the analytic–synthetic statement distinction is discussed in Chapter 6 of Findlay's book *Meinong's Theory of Objects and Values*.

object can have characteristics though it does not have being.[35] The earlier discussion in this section points to the formal way of putting this version of the principle of independence; the argument

> There is a property P such that P is possessed by s;
> So, s has being

is invalid. This explication of the principle seems particularly appropriate if, following Chisholm, it is read as saying that an object can have characteristics even though it has no being.[36]

This looser version of the principle of independence differs from the strict version in two key respects. First, no mention of a *set* of properties (a *Sosein*) *attaching* to an object occurs in instances of the looser version; mention is made only of properties and their *possession* by objects. Second, the properties satisfying particular instances of the looser version can be extranuclear in contrast to the strict version. Thus, *because* the property of being fictional is the epitome of an extranuclear property, the loose version of the principle of independence, but not the strict version, could be used to justify the claim that arguments such as that from 'Sherlock Holmes has the property of being a possible object' to 'Sherlock Holmes subsists' are not valid[37] simply by virtue of Sherlock Holmes *having* the property of being a possible object.

Consider the statement just introduced, that P is possessed by s. The substituents of 'P' are property designators, that is, singular terms such as 'being spherical', 'roundness', and so on. So one would expect, in an orderly development of Meinong's principle of independence, the evidence cited for that principle to be in language such as 'Roundness is a property of the round square but the round square does not

---

[35] Thus, e.g., Chisholm's rendition; *Realism and the Background of Phenomenology*, p. 25, and Findlay's statement in *Meinong's Theory of Objects and Values*, 2nd edn, p. 44.

[36] *Realism and the Background of Phenomenology*, p. 25. Here 'P' and 's' again take as values, respectively, properties and objects.

[37] Meinong, 'On the Theory of Objects', p. 82. Chisholm, and his colleagues, seem to be aware of the strict and loose versions of the principle of independence because they write in their translators' note on the same page of this source that a 'rough' translation for an object's *Sosein* is 'its having characteristics'.

subsist', or, perhaps, even more carefully, in language such as 'Roundness is possessed by the round square but the round square does not subsist'. But seldom is this consistently done either by Meinong or by his disciples and expositors. Rather, the evidence is usually expressed in language such as: The round square is round but the round square does not exist. Here the relational expressions 'is a property of' and 'is possessed by' are missing and the singular term 'roundness' is replaced by the *general term* 'round'. Meinong, his disciples and his expositors slip back and forth between the two modes of expression quite innocently, seemingly because of the tacit assumption that, for instance, the general term 'round' applies truly to those things having what the singular term 'roundness' designates, and thus apparently without concern either for the difference in logical form of the two statements 'Roundness is possessed by the round square' and 'The round square is round', or for the possible difference in ontic function in the two modes of expression a Quineian is likely to stress; that it is by way of 'roundness' that one refers to the property (if such there be), never by way of the general term 'round', is something no Meinongian ever worried about, nor is it clear that he need have.

In the rest of this essay nothing turns on whether the strict or loose version of the principle of independence is used. Since the looser version is simpler and also affords continuity between the authorities and the current work, it will henceforth be adopted. This means leaving behind the nuclear–extranuclear property distinction vital to Meinong's theory. For the present purposes it is sufficient to have pointed out why and how that distinction is important to the Meinongian scheme of things.

It is interesting to consider how the principle of independence, strictly or loosely interpreted, affects Meinong's position *vis à vis* Descartes' famous historical maxim about being, that to be is to have a property. Clearly this is not an acceptable maxim from Meinong's perspective. A more accurate maxim, and one more acceptable to those seeking a less psychological statement about what objects are in Meinong's theory, replaces 'to be' by the expression 'to be an object' in Descartes' maxim.

Reflection on the difference between the strict and loose versions of the principle of independence, however, raises an important philosophical question about the Meinongian maxim: *to be an object* is to have a property. What I mean is this. Strict adherence to Meinongian parlance and conceptions also seems to support another maxim: to be an object is to have a nature. Whether the 'looser' maxim about objecthood entails the latter maxim is the question of whether an object can have properties but no nature, whether, for example, an object can have the property of nonbeing but no nature. Meinong's notion of 'defective objects' makes the question a tantalizing and difficult one: whether the defective object which is the thought about a thought not about itself has any nature at all, though having *no being* is not an easy matter to decide.[38]

Another question of interest is whether other Meinongian principles are reasonably susceptible of reconstruction in the present style. Of course, whether the answer is 'yes' or 'no' does not affect the plausibility of the present construal of the principle of independence. There is no reason why a philosophical theory cannot contain different *sorts* of principle, some perhaps logical in nature, others, say, more ontological. So the current question is motivated by curiosity, given the aim of this book. Once it is asked, the answer seems clearly 'yes'. For example, the principle of indifference might be fairly expressed in the strict idiom as follows: the statement that neither being nor nonbeing is a member of the set of nuclear properties P_1, P_2 ... attaching to object s is logically true. One may now inquire whether, under this construal of the principle of indifference, the two principles imply one another, whether in a common sense of 'logical independence', the principles are mutually independent, or whether one or the other is merely a conse-

---

[38] See A. Meinong, *Über emotionale Präsentation* (*On Emotional Presentation*), Report of the Kaiserliche Akademie der Wissenschaften (Vienna, 1917), trans. M.-L Schubert Kalsi; Northwestern University Press, Evanston, Ill., 1972.

quence and not a basic principle of the Meinongian edifice. As far as I can see the answer is that they are quite independent. For the fact that the nonbeing of Pegasus is not logically implied by the nature of Pegasus gives one no information about what Pegasus is – about what makes Pegasus the object he is. And conversely, that (say) the nonbeing of the round square is not part of its nature, does not give one any information about whether it is logically implied or not logically implied by its nature, though presumably if a property is part of the nature of an object, possession of that property is implied by its nature. To put the matter briefly, the question of *what* is in the nature of an object is independent of the question of *when* the object has a nature.

IV. MORE ON INDEPENDENCE

Elsewhere the principle of independence has been expressed as the principle that the 'is' of predication does not imply the 'is' of being.[39] The relation between this statement of the principle of independence, and the interpretation of that principle in the preceding section may be explained in various ways. Perhaps the clearest explanation is as follows.

Both Meinong and the tradition he opposes regard a statement as having the logical form of a predication just in case it can be represented (or paraphrased) as a statement of the form 'The property P is possessed by (object) s.' Take the statement 'The round square is round', for example. It is a predication for Meinong because it is paraphraseable as 'The property of being round is possessed by the round square'. Russell would have objected to the example but not to the conception of predication.

The tradition that Meinong opposes considers the argument

> There is a property P that P is possessed by s;
> So, s is (has being)

---

[39] Karel Lambert, 'Being and Being So', in *Jenseits von Sein und Nichtsein*, pp. 37–46.

to be valid. It also accepts as valid the argument

The property Q is possessed by s;
So, there is a property P such that P is possessed by s.

So, for that tradition, the statement 'The round square is round' implies the statement 'The round square is (has being)': the 'is' of predication implies the 'is' of being in two brief inferential steps. Faced with the falsity of the consequent of this implication, the traditional response would be to deny the truth of the antecedent. But Meinong believed the antecedent statement to be true, recording a fact as 'hard' as that recorded by the predication 'Kant is a philosopher.' So he boldly denied that a statement about an object implied the being of that object simply in virtue of its being a predication. Considerations such as these inevitably led him to reject the validating character of the first of the pair of argument patterns above, and thus ultimately to espouse the principle of independence.

A final point about predication is in order here. The phrase 'the "is" of predication' is ambiguous. It may mean, first, that the word 'is' in 'Meinong is profound' purports to express a relation – the relation of predication – alleged to hold between the attribute of being profound (or, if one wishes, the attributive general term 'profound') and the object named 'Meinong', and, second, that the word 'is' in the statement 'Meinong is profound' signifies that that statement has a certain *logical form* or, as Quine puts it, exhibits a certain 'construction', called 'predication'.

Meinong could have subscribed to both interpretations of the phrase since in his theory they are virtually equivalent. But they are only equivalent in the presence of at least the semantical requirement that every singular term has a bearer, a requirement Meinong apparently did adopt.[40] For example,

---

[40] A few words have to be said here about Russell's famous 'demolition' of objects having no being, and thus of the view that definite descriptions such as 'the gold mountain' and 'the round square' and grammatically proper names such as 'Ichabod Crane' 'stand for' beingless objects. Russell himself believed that the foundations of Meinong's entire theory rested on footings consisting of beingless objects,

the claim that the statement 'Pegasus is impulsive' has the logical form of a predication does not imply that the word 'is' in that statement expresses a certain relation alleged to hold between 'impulsive' and the object named 'Pegasus', because, traditional opinion to the contrary, there is (or should be)

among which impossible objects were nothing less than crucial. Thus in his 'Review of A. Meinong's *Untersuchungen zur Gegenstandstheorie und Psychologie*', (*Mind*, NS 14 (1905), p. 537) Russell writes disarmingly:

> It is not customary for philosophers to face the round square with so much courage; and indeed few logicians can withstand its onset. But if we are to be clear about the supposed nonsubsistent objects, it is quite essential that we should have a theory about the round square.

Graduate students from 1905 on have participated vicariously in Russell's destruction of the Meinongian edifice, usually with the open glee of an architectural critic at contemplating the annihilation of Disneyland. Russell's argument, as scholars know, is contained in a brief passage in his remarkable essay 'On Denoting' in Robert C. Marsh (ed.), *Logic and Knowledge* (Allen and Unwin, London, 1956), p. 45:

> This theory [Meinong's] regards any grammatically correct denoting phrase as standing for an *object*. Thus 'the present King of France', 'the round square', etc., are supposed to be genuine objects. It is admitted that such objects do not *subsist*, but nevertheless they are supposed to be objects. This is in itself a difficult view; but the chief objection is that such objects, admittedly are apt to infringe the law of contradiction. It is contended, for example, that the existent present King of France exists, and also does not exist; that the round square is round, and also not round, etc. ... But this is intolerable...

Meinong had responses to this argument, some of which have received renewed credibility in Terence Parsons' reconstruction of Meinong's theory; see Terence Parsons, 'A Prolegomena to Meinongian Semantics', *Journal of Philosophy*, 71 (1974), pp. 561–80. But even if one were to find these Meinongian responses, either original or reconstructed, ultimately unsatisfactory, the fact still remains that Russell's claim to have demolished beingless objects is just wrong. (See Karel Lambert, 'Impossible Objects', *Inquiry*, 17 (1974), pp. 303–14, and R. Routley, 'On "The Durability of Impossible Objects"', *Inquiry*, 19 (1976), pp. 247–51, and my reply therein.) The most Russell showed is that certain principles of Meinong's theory would have to be given up, assuming the sanctity of standard first order predicate logic. For example, a principle alluded to earlier (and which ought to be dubbed the principle of *Sosein* – the principle that if a property is part of an object's nature, then the object possesses it) clearly is jeopardized by Russell's considerations about the round square. On the other hand, the import of Russell's criticism, even when thus confined, should not be underestimated. For if the principle of *Sosein* is false, the questions arise, What can be truly or falsely said of beingless objects? and, What are the grounds for such claims? If no such principle is forthcoming, one can then justifiably wonder about the value of accepting the beingless, whether, for example, the round square football is 'there' to mull over, let alone to kick around any more. And given the well-known cumulative effect of wonderings, one would then be led to wonder seriously whether such singular terms as 'the round square' (or 'the round square football') and 'Ichabod Crane' successfully refer after all, in the wide sense of the term 'refer'.

nothing in the notion of the logical form of a predication demanding that the expression 'Pegasus' refer to an object of any kind. At least there appears to be no more justification for this presumption than there is for the presumption that the general term 'flying horse' in the predicational statement 'Pegasus is a flying horse' is true of some objects. So the second reading of the phrase 'the "is" of predication' is weaker than the first in the sense that it does not require the subject term to refer whereas the first interpretation does.

Let me turn to another point. Many contemporary philosophical logicians interpret 'reference' more narrowly than Meinong, requiring an existent as bearer – or at least a subsistent when the narrower Meinongian sense of 'exist' is intended – if there is to be successful reference by a singular term. For them, *contra* Meinong, the expression 'the gold mountain' does not refer. Further, among these logicians there are some that nevertheless hold simple statements such as 'The gold mountain = the gold mountain' to be true. So these logicians, a species of positive free logician,[41] agree with Meinong about the truth-value of the example sentence, but differ with him about the referring status of the constituent singular term 'the gold mountain', the former holding that it refers but to a nonsubsistent object, and the latter that it does not refer at all though it purports to do so. (Here nonreference to a subsistent object is explained by using the principle that 't' refers to a subsistent if and only if it is true that t has being, where t is a singular term. For example, the expression

---

[41] Free logics for present purposes can be divided into two classes according to their policies on the truth-values of simple (or atomic) statements containing irreferential singular terms, in the narrower sense of 'irreferential' described above. Thus a free logic in which every simple statement containing an irreferential singular term (*a*) is false or (*b*) is truth-valueless may be called *negative free logics*; otherwise they are *positive free logics*. An example of a negative free logic of the first kind is Tyler Burge's version in 'Truth and Singular Terms', *Noûs* 8 (1975), pp. 309–25, and of the second kind, one of Brian Skyrms' versions in 'Supervaluations: Identity, Existence, and Individual Concepts', *The Journal of Philosophy*, 16 (1968), pp. 477–83. An example of a positive free logic is Dana Scott's rendition in 'Existence and Description in Formal Logic'. This essay appears in R. Schoenman (ed.), *Bertrand Russell: Philosopher of the Century* (George Allen and Unwin, London, 1967), pp. 181–200. A fuller discussion of free logic, and certain of its subtleties, is undertaken later.

'Meinong' refers to a subsistent just because it is true that Meinong has being.) There is also agreement that the statement in question can be true, though 'The gold mountain exists (or has being)' is false. So the important fact that emerges is that both certain positive free logicians and Meinongians acknowledge the Mally–Meinong principle of independence, or rather a consequence of it.

V. ON MEINONG'S MOTIVATION FOR THE THEORY OF (COMPLETE) OBJECTS

There remains one issue in this cursory introduction to Meinong's theory of (complete) objects and its distinctive principle of independence: Why did he feel the theory so compelling despite its unusual – indeed admittedly bizarre – character?[42] Of course, such a question need not, and does not here, arise from curiosity about the distinctive character of Meinong's psyche, fascinating and scientifically fruitful though that kind of inquiry might prove to be. Rather it is occasioned by the desire to understand the philosophical concerns Meinong thought required the postulation of non-subsistent objects and the adoption of certain principles governing them, in particular the principle of independence.

It is often said that Meinong was led to his theory by what he took to be the correct analysis of psychological acts. True, but this does not get at the deeper roots of Meinong's convictions, into which the concern with psychological acts falls as a quite natural part. The deeper motive, one which Meinong does allude to now and then, but usually is content to let play out its influence behind the scenes, can be expressed simply as the concern to explain how what he took to be clearly true statements, for example 'The *perpetuum mobile* is nonexistent' (in the broad and univocal sense Quine attaches to the word

---

[42] Meinong was quite prepared for the dropping of jaws that exposure to his radical conceptions would, and did, produce. Findlay reports in *Meinong's Theory of Objects and Values*, p. 44, for example, that Meinong admitted the principle of independence to be 'very difficult to stomach, but [thought] that this is solely due to our prejudice in favor of the actual'.

'nonexistent'), 'The round square is round', and 'Goldberg thinks of the *perpetuum mobile*', can be true. Especially note-worthy is the last example. Meinong, letting grammar be his guide, took it to express a relationship, and in part to be about a psychological act, the act of thought (or thinking). Hence the observation above that the concern with psychological acts is but a special case of a more general concern.[43] Similarly, he took the statements 'The round square is round' and 'The *perpetuum mobile* is nonexistent' to express attributions. It was quite natural, then, for Meinong to conclude that 'the round square' and 'the *perpetuum mobile*' stand for objects. For how otherwise could the truth of the statements above be accoun-ted for? Relations do require things to relate and attributions do require things to have the attributes. The important question had to do with the character of these objects.

Under the influence of Brentano and Twardowski, Meinong rejected the view that the objects in question were really certain kinds of mental entities, or more broadly, intentional objects of any kind.[44] In the first place, the objects in question may be nonpsychical whereas entities with which some allege them to be the same are psychical, and in the second place, these same mental entities exist, and thus have being, though the objects in question do not have being. Nor did Meinong find plausible a position which some allege his mentor Brentano to have taken when he held – anticipating Russell in certain respects – that the problem of the character of the *perpe-*

[43] It is interesting that Chisholm, in his defense of Meinong's theory in *Jenseits von Sein und Nichtsein*, pp. 27–33, is guided by the question, 'What is the best way to explain the truth of certain statements having specified logical forms?' I think that such a question also underlies Meinong's own reflections, though he may have not phrased it so. One need only remember Meinong's injunction 'that the general theory of objects must learn from grammar' (see above, p. 2) to see the aptness of this analysis of the basic source of Meinongian motives.

[44] Twardowski apparently rejected these identifications by ingenious and clear appli-cations of the discernability of nonidenticals. Recently Rheinhard Grossmann has translated into English the most important work of the apparent precursor of the Polish school of logic; and for this monoglot English-speaking philosophers must be greatly indebted to him. Twardowski's is an especially clear and profound mind, and deserves to be 'discovered' by Anglo-American scholars. (See K. Twardowski, *On The Content and Object of Presentations*, translated by R. Grossman; Martinus Nijhoff, The Hague, 1977.)

tuum mobile and the round square is ill-founded because it rests on the questionable presumptions that 'The *perpetuum mobile* is nonexistent' and 'The round square is round' express attributions and 'Goldberg thinks of the *perpetuum mobile*' expresses a relationship. Meinong would surely have felt that Brentano's position simply reflected a prejudice in favor of the actual. So, given Meinong's views on the logical form of statements containing what contemporary philosophical logicians call irreferential singular terms, his postulation of nonsubsistent objects to account for the truth of certain statements seems quite sensible, and certainly more so than the psychologistic-looking alternative which appeals to various creatures in the intentionalia *Tiergarten* as the relata of certain relations and the objects of certain attributions. Meinong's position on complete objecta can be summed up thus: he accepted the traditional logical doctrine of terms, and, to paraphrase Ryle, both generalized the issues and remorselessly drew the conclusions of that doctrine that others of fainter heart could neither confront nor accept. Nor is it true that Meinong's theory of nonsubsistent objects is 'dead, buried and not going to be resurrected'.[45] In fact it has been resurrected in different guises in contemporary philosophical logic, and at least one recent book champions something very much like it,[46] thus belying the wide belief that Meinong's doctrine rests on trivial grammatical confusions which, had they not been taken seriously by its inventor, would perhaps have come to be seen as subtle philosophical puns.[47]

[45] See G. Ryle, 'Intentionality – Theory and the Nature of Thinking' in *Jenseits von Sein und Nichtsein*, p. 7.

[46] Terence Parsons, *Nonexistent Objects*.

[47] This remark, originally directed at Hegel, was expropriated from Russell's *Our Knowledge of the External World* (Norton, New York, 1929), p. 42.

3

INDEPENDENCE AND
PREDICATION: I

I. THE PRINCIPLE OF INDEPENDENCE AND PREDICATION

The question of which statements are predications has been, and continues to be, one of the foremost of analytic philosophy. It was almost an obsession with Russell; the wrong answer to this question, he believed, led absolute idealism astray, and also drove Meinong to an extreme brand of realism which could not but offend anyone with 'a robust sense of reality'. It is a matter of at least historical importance, then, what Meinong's answer to this question was, and how that answer was influenced by the principle of independence.

That the principle of independence directly concerns the concept of predication will be obvious from the last chapter. But there whether a statement expressed a predication was seen as a question about whether that statement could be paraphrased legitimately into talk of possession and properties, a popular way of seeing the question especially in the earlier half of this century. Whether the statement 'The non-spherical spheroid is spherical' qualifies as a predication is the question whether it is correctly paraphrased as a statement in a formal or artificial language which may be read as 'The spheroid which is such that it is not a spheroid possesses the property of being spherical (sphericity)'. Meinong would have answered yes, Russell no.

In the last two decades talk about the concept of predication has been refined – or at least redefined. The new theoretical idiom is much more appropriate to the logical cast given to so many traditional philosophical problems in analytic philosophy. Rather than talk of properties (nonlinguistic things), there is talk of general and singular terms (linguistic things), and rather than talk of relations like possession, there is talk of relations like being true of (or application). So a major topic of interest in this chapter is how Meinong's views appear in the new idiom, in what may be called the semantical mode.

What is the connection between Meinong's principle of independence and his theory of predication? For that matter, what is a theory of predication in the first place? Here, the answer to the latter question is straightforward enough: a theory of predication is a theory about what particular logical form predication is. The answer to the former question, the explanation of which is the main topic of this chapter, in broad outline is this.

There is a respect in which Meinong's theory differs not one iota from either Russell's theory or Frege's (as manifested in Frege's conception of scientific language). This respect is what will be called the *core* of the traditional theory of predication. Roughly it says that the truth-value of a predication depends on whether what is said of the object specified by its singular term (or terms) is true (or false) of that object (or objects). However, there is also an important *constraint* on the traditional theory adopted by Russell and Frege, but rejected by Meinong. It says, roughly, that the objects specified in a predication must have being. (Undoubtedly the traditional theory of predication has other important principles, but for the purposes of this essay, the traditional theory refers, for brevity, to the theory composed of the core principle and the constraint just described.) So at the core, Meinong's theory is completely traditional. A predisposing reason for the distinction between core and constraint is the fact that there is a nontraditional theory of predication – the subject of the next chapter – in a version of which the principle of independence fails, and in another of which it holds.

Meinong's theory of predication is therefore not a complete break from the traditional theory of predication, the theory manifested in Russell's various discussions of logical form – at least through 'The Philosophy of Logical Atomism' – and also in Frege's philosophy of scientific language. At first glance, this may seem a preposterous conclusion given the different verdicts of Meinong and Russell on statements such as

(1) The round square is round,
(2) The sun god is powerful,

and

(3) Mill thinks of the round square.

Russell would have judged (1)–(3) to be nonpredicational, but not Meinong. At second glance, the conclusion in question may not seem so preposterous after all when one considers that Frege's verdicts on (1)–(3) agree exactly with Meinong. The feeling of preposterousness, in short, arises from a failure to distinguish between the questions of what Meinong's and Russell's theories of predication are, and which statements qualify as predications for Meinong and Russell.

Before getting down to the substance of the claims in the previous pair of paragraphs, certain preliminaries concerning predication have to be settled. First, the statements which can have the logical form of predication are singular statements. They are statements containing at least one logically isolable expression purporting to refer to one and only one object – a *singular term*; the statement 'Zatopek runs' is an example. Hence, as the word 'predication' is here used, the traditional subject–predicate statements of the medieval square of opposition cannot be predications *unless* they contain at least one singular term. (The concept of singular term will be examined at greater length shortly.) Second, relational singular statements can be predications. In this, the precedent is Quine's treatment, and for the same reason – convenience.[1] Thus, 'Zatopek is faster than Nurmi' is predicational – or more accurately is a kind of statement that can be predicational. Third, predicational statements can be simple or complex. For the moment presuming them to be predicational, 'Zatopek runs'

[1] W. V. Quine, *Word and Object* (Wiley, New York, 1960), p. 106.

and 'Zatopek is faster than Nurmi' would be examples of simple predications, whereas 'Zatopek is a tireless runner' and 'Zatopek is a more determined runner than Nurmi' would be complex predications.[2]

II. THE TRADITIONAL THEORY OF PREDICATION

'Predication' specifies a certain kind of logical form. But what is logical form? The conception implicit in Quine's *Word and Object*, and explicit in David Kaplan's essay 'What Is Russell's Theory of Descriptions?',[3] is the one that will be adopted here. The main feature of the Kaplan–Quine view is that the notion of logical form is a *semantical* notion. The idea is that the logical form of a statement consists in the *way* it is evaluated for truth-value. Kaplan's own statement of the semantic conception of logical form, a statement intended only as a heuristic device for gleaning the essence of Russell's theory of definite descriptions and not as the ultimate expression of a finished view, is worth quoting:

> The logical form of a sentence should mirror its grammatical form. The grammar of a language is assumed to be given in terms of certain grammatical categories such as term, formula, two-place predicate,

---

[2] A rigorous technical treatment of predicational constructions would have to include some device for making predicates – for instance, Leonard's dot operator, which when placed over a variable fabricates n-placed general terms (or predicates) out of open sentences. (See H. S. Leonard, 'Essences, Attributes and Predicates', presidential address, 62nd Annual Meeting of the Western Division of the American Philosophical Association, Milwaukee, 1964.) To illustrate, by means of this device, the open sentence 'x runs' yields the 1-place general term '$(\dot{x})(x$ runs$)$', and the open sentence 'x is faster than y' yields the 2-place general term '$(\dot{x})(\dot{y})(x$ is faster than $y)$'. Predicational statements then could be represented as follows: '$(\dot{x})(x$ runs$)$ Zatopek' and '$(\dot{x})(\dot{y})(x$ is faster than $y)$ Zatopek, Nurmi' are simple predications. Complex predications would depend on the presence of a logical operator in the general term or predicate; thus 'Zatopek is a tireless runner' might get represented as '$(\dot{x})(x$ is a runner and x is tireless$)$ Zatopek', 'Zatopek is a more determined runner than Nurmi' as $(\dot{x})(\dot{y})(x$ is a runner and y is a runner and x is more determined than $y)$ Zatopek, Nurmi', and 'Zatopek is someone' as '$(\dot{x})((Ey)(y$ is a person and $y=x))$ Zatopek'. The syntax in part thus would be similar to that in the representation of function or property talk via Church's lambda operator 'λ'. The major difference is that the lambda operator yields singular terms from open sentences whereas the dot operator produces general terms.

[3] In W. Yourgrau *et al.*, *Physics, Logic and History*, Plenum Press, New York, 1970.

etc. Each atomic expression is assigned to some such category, and *formation rules* are given which tell us how we can form compounds of a given grammatical category from components of certain grammatical categories. The grammatical form of an expression is then determined by the formation rules. An expression is grammatically correct if it can be 'constructed' from grammatically simple components in accordance with the formation rules. Such a construction assigns a grammatical structure, or form, to the expression. To parse a sentence is to exhibit its grammatical form. Just as grammatical properties and relations, such as being a noun clause or being the subject of a given sentence, depend on the grammatical form of the expression in question, so logical properties and relations, such as being valid or being a logical consequence of a given sentence, depend on the logical form of the expressions in question. Logical form is determined by the *evaluation rules* of the language. These rules tell us how to 'construct' the semantical value of an expression in terms of the values of its logically simple components. (We here take the semantical value to be what Carnap calls 'the extension', that is: a truth value for sentences, an individual for names, a class of individuals for one-place predicates, and so on.) Such a construction of the truth value of a sentence exhibits the logical structure, or form, of the sentence in a way analogous to that in which parsing a sentence exhibits its grammatical form.[4]

That Quine's own view of predicational constructions is in the spirit of Kaplan is evident in his characterization of predication in *Word and Object*.[5] There he speaks of a statement containing a 1-place general term being a predication just in case its truth-value is determined in a certain way – that is, by determining whether a certain relation – the relation 'true (or false) of' – holds between constituent general term and specified object.

The core of the traditional theory of predication, in Quineian language, is that a statement *has the logical form of predication just in case it consists of an* n-*place general term joined to* n

---

[4] *Ibid.*, p. 283. This conception of logical form, though perhaps defective as a complete answer to the question, 'What is logical form?'. surely is in the right direction. In the next chapter a limitation on Kaplan's theory will indeed be discussed. But the concerns of this chapter are not affected by that limitation.

[5] Pp. 96 and 106.

singular terms and is true (or false) according as that general term is true (or false) of the n-tuple of objects specified by the n singular terms, or of the object specified by the singular term if n = *1*. (n is greater than or equal to 1.) The core principle of predication so expressed will be designated CT. It is worth emphasizing that in CT *all* singular terms must refer to objects.

An explanation of the key expressions in this statement of CT is in order. First, the word 'joined' in CT tolerates both concatenation of general terms and singular terms and copulative infixing, as in, respectively, 'Zatopek runs', 'Zatopek is tireless' (or 'Zatopek is a runner'). Second, a *general term* is an expression purporting to be true or false of each entity, if any at all, in a given class. Thus, 'runner', 'won the 5,000 meters in such and such Olympic games', 'runner on Jupiter' and 'runs faster than' are all general terms. Some are simple ('runner'), and some are complex ('runner on Jupiter'); some are true of some objects in a given class ('runner'), others are true of no objects in a given class ('runner on Jupiter'); and some are false of some objects in a given class ('runner') and others false of every object in a given class ('runner on Jupiter'). A rough and ready rule of thumb for picking out general terms is this: if an article can be significantly prefixed to an expression, or to the expression plus the word 'thing', the expression is a general term – as in 'a man' and 'the pretty thing'. Contrast these cases with the nonsignificant 'an all roads lead to Rome', establishing that 'all roads lead to Rome' is not a general term.[6] Third, a *singular term* is an expression purporting to refer to one and only one object. Examples are 'that snow is white', 'Meinong', 'the round square', '2' and 'being a *perpetuum mobile*'. Some are simple ('Meinong'), some are complex ('the round square'); and some are referential ('Meinong'), and, in the minds of many contemporary philosophers, but not Meinong's, some are irreferential ('Vulcan', 'the round square').[7]

---

[6] This rough device is Leonard's. See his *Principles of Reasoning*.

[7] The word 'purport' in these explanations of 'singular term' and 'general term' signals, however vaguely, the logical roles the two kinds of term play in statements.

Further, and, finally, the expressions 'true' and 'true of' (and, correspondingly, 'false' and 'false of') have quite different uses, the former expressing a nonrelational feature of statements, and the latter a relation between parts of statements and objects. Of course, the two kinds of uses are paired in predications. For example, assuming the statement 'Meinong thinks' to be a predication, then CT asserts that statement to be *true* in virtue of the fact that the general term 'thinks' is *true of* Meinong (or of the object specified by the singular term 'Meinong'); and vice versa. Similarly, assuming the statement 'Meinong played baseball' to be a predication, then CT licenses that statement to be *false* because the general term 'played baseball' is *false of* Meinong (or the object specified by the singular term 'Meinong'); and vice versa.

With the terminology explained, a puzzle arises about the traditional theory of predication given CT. CT states what has been referred to earlier as the core of the traditional theory of predication. It speaks unqualifiedly of objects, but the theory of which it is the core recognizes no subjects of predication but *subsistent objects* (or existent objects in Quine's sense of 'existent'). How so, if not in the core of theory? The answer is: because of an important constraint on the traditional theory,

---

The idea in the case of singular terms, for example, is that they function like logical pronouns – like free individual *variables* (as opposed to *parameters*) in classical predicate logic. That is, they function like those logical expressions, variables, whose purpose it is to specify the topic of concern toward which the rest of the statement is directed, and not like those logical expressions, parameters, that serve as placeholders for constants. (The two uses are conflated in the treatment of variables in most standard logic texts, but not by Richmond Thomason – for instance – in his book *Symbolic Logic* (Macmillan, New York, 1970). Pedantic precision is not the goal; for the distinction when made explicit yields a simplification in the statement of certain logical rules.) Such a use of variables does not require that they succeed in specifying, though in most logic texts that additional demand is usually placed on variables. In the case of general terms there is a difference. In contrast to singular terms they do not function like logical pronouns at all but only like parameters, and only *predicate* parameters at that. General terms are not referring kinds of expression at all, and thus their logical role is not properly explained by appeal to logical pronouns, variables, be they individual variables or some other kind of variable. Their correlative abstract nouns, of course, do function like variables. For example, 'honesty' functions like a variable, but the general term 'honest' does not; the former refers (perhaps) to an attribute, but the latter is *true of* just those things having that attribute. In these matters I follow Quine (see *Word and Object*, pp. 240–1).

the constraint that the singular terms of a predication refer to subsistent objects – or equivalently, that the predication implies that the objects specified by those singular terms have being. This constraint rarely receives explicit mention in the traditional theory, though Russell comes close to it in *Principia Mathematica*. There, in the first part of his argument by cases that definite descriptions are inccomplete symbols, he writes:

If we supply a context, as in 'Socrates is mortal', these words express a fact of which Socrates himself is a constituent: there is a certain object, namely Socrates, which does have the property of immortality, and this object is a constituent of the complex fact which we assert when we say 'Socrates is mortal.' But in other cases this simple analysis fails us. Suppose we say: 'The round square does not exist.' It seems plain that this is a true proposition, yet *we cannot regard it as denying the existence of a certain object called 'the round square'. For if there were such an object, it would exist* . . .[8]

And, of course, the constraint is vigorously defended in Russell's *Introduction to Mathematical Philosophy*, where his state-ment of what predication is in spirit virtually duplicates the account expressed here (though not its terminology), and his famous espousal of a robust sense of reality grounds the con-straint.[9] That constraint is reflected there in the claims that the subject of a predication can be specified only by a (logi-cally) proper name, and a proper name must refer to a 'real object' (i.e. a subsistent object in the current sense of 'subsi-stent').

Usually the constraint does its work as a presupposition in particular instances of the theory of predication recently expressed. Frege, who surely would have found the spirit of the traditional theory congenial if not its language, is a case in point. He believed in the existence of singular terms in natural language that refer to nothing – 'Odysseus', for example, but for reasons of logical perfection required all singular terms in

[8] A. Whitehead and B. Russell, *Principia Mathematica* (2nd edn, The University Press, Cambridge, 1925), p. 66; my italics.

[9] B. Russell, *Introduction to Mathematical Philosophy*, George Allen and Unwin, London, 1919. See especially pp. 141–3, and the chapter entitled 'Descriptions'.

the scientific language to refer to objects; 0, according to one method, and a certain set of objects, according to the other method. It is precisely at this juncture that the constraint plays its surreptitious role; for neither sets nor 0 are non-subsistent objects for Frege.

The word 'constraint' deserves more sober consideration. It has about it the sense of ruling out or blocking refractory cases, cases that are theoretically embarrassing. In the present case, if Russell is to be believed, the admission of beingless referents for certain singular terms threatens the law of noncontradiction given that statements such as 'The spheroid which is such that it is not a spheroid is spherical'. 'The spheroid which is such that it is not a spheroid is not spherical' and 'The existent king of the United States is an existent' are predications. This argument and other horrors attendant on beingless referents in predications are detailed in the *Introduction to Mathematical Philosophy*.[10]

In the terminology of this chapter, Russell's argument apparently is as follows. Suppose, for example, the spheroid which is such that it is not a spheroid is allowed to float to the ontic surface and taken to be what the expression 'the spheroid which is such that it is not a spheroid' specifies in the statement 'The spheroid which is such that it is not a spheroid is spherical.' On the natural (non-Fregeian) assumption that the object specified by 'the spheroid which is such that it is not a spheroid' is an object of which the *basis* of this definite description (the 'so and so' part of 'the so and so') is true, then surely the general term 'spherical' is true of the spheroid which is such that it is not a spheroid.[11] But if the statement in question

---

[10] *Ibid.*, chapter entitled 'Descriptions'. It is historically interesting that Russell's argument here is quite different from his argument in 'On Denoting' that Meinong's theory of beingless objects leads to contradiction. The argument in 'On Denoting', taken literally, is invalid – as mentioned in the previous chapter.

[11] In his essay 'Frege and Russell on Vacuous Singular Terms', in Matthias Scheru (ed.), *Studies on Frege*, III: *Logic and Semantics* (Friedrich Fromman Verlag, Gunther Holzboog, 1976), p. 110, Leonard Linsky says that contradiction is an immediate consequence of the designation rule that 'the so and so' denotes the so and so. However, as the discussion above shows, more is needed; at the very least, the requirement that 'so and so' in 'the so and so' is true of the so and so.

is a predication, then it is true. By parity of reasoning, as Russell would say, it also follows that the statement 'The spheroid which is such that it is not a spheroid is not spherical (= nonspherical)' is true because the general term 'nonspherical' is also true of the spheroid which is such that it is not a spheroid. So the law of noncontradiction is jeopardized.

Again following Russell's somewhat misleading presentation, consider the subsistent king of the United States, a possible but beingless object. By reasoning similar to that in the previous paragraph the truth of 'The subsistent king of the United States is a subsistent' can be established, given that that statement is a predication, because, again, the general term 'subsistent' is true of the subsistent king of the United States. On the other hand, since in fact no such object is subsistent, it follows also that the predication 'The subsistent king of the United States is not subsistent' is true, again frustrating the law of noncontradiction.

Talk of constraints to avoid conflict with alleged logical laws has been much in the forefront of recent philosophical logic. It is now a commonplace that a constraint on the account of logical truth one finds in most current intermediate logic texts is that singular terms refer to existent (subsistent) objects, or, for example, the *principle of specification* fails. The principle of specification is the logical principle that the statement that every existent object is so and so logically implies the statement that s is so and so where 's' takes as substituends singular terms, and 'so and so' general terms. But substitution of 'exists' for 'so and so' and 'Pegasus' for 's' violates the principle. Hence the present constraint. Similarly with the constraint on the traditional theory of predication: the motive is to save logical theory – or so Russell believed. And it is his discussion which has assumed the aura of Holy Writ among the analytically devout.

III. MEINONG'S CONCEPTION OF PREDICATION

Meinong's theory of predication is best reconstructed as

simply CT minus the traditional constraint. This characterization exhibits both what he and Russell (and Frege), held in common – that, for example, in a genuine predication the singular terms had to successfully refer to an object. It also exhibits how he differed from Russell (and Frege) – in that, for example, the objects referred to by those singular terms need not be subsistent.

Earlier the distinctive feature of Meinong's conception of predication was previewed as the lifting of the traditional constraint, that such indeed is the direct effect of adoption of the principle of independence. The argument for that claim can be put as follows.

Consider first the simplest kind of predication, a statement containing only a single occurrence of a singular term – say, 'Meinong thinks', for instance. The form of this statement may be expressed as

(4) Gs,

where 'G' takes as substituends general terms ('thinks', for example) and 's' takes as substituends singular terms ('Meinong', for example). To say that 'Gs' is the form of a predication is to say that any statement composed of a general term and a singular term ('Meinong thinks') has its truth-value, truth or falsity, computed according as the general term replacing 'G' ('thinks') is true or false of the object specified by the singular term replacing 's' ('Meinong'). In the previous chapter 'Meinong thinks' qualified as a predication on different grounds. There the measure was paraphrased into a statement of the form 'P is possessed by s', where the substituends of 'P' and 's' are both singular terms.

Doubtless many, including Meinong, would have felt few qualms about believing that if a statement qualified as a predication directly (via the method of the current chapter), it would also qualify indirectly (via the method of the previous chapter). Indeed, there is ample reason to believe that because of the conviction earlier imputed to him that general terms ('thinks') are true of exactly those objects possessing the property denoted by the (correlative) singular term ('(the property of) being a thinker'), Meinong surely would have embraced the logical equivalence of 'Gs' and 'P is possessed by s' where 'P' takes as substituends the correlative singular terms of the general terms which are substituends of 'G'. This equivalence is used in the argument that the principle of independence entails rejection of the traditional constraint that the singular terms of a predication, in the direct sense, refer to subsistent objects, to existents (in Quine's sense of the term).

So, and secondly, consider again the traditional constraint: the singular terms of a predication (in the direct sense) refer to objects having being (subsistents). Given the understanding about reference enunciated in Section IV of Chapter 2 – that the singular term 's' refers to a subsistent just in case it is true that s has being – the traditional constraint amounts to licensing the validity of

(5) Gs;
      So, s has being

(in the simplest case where there is only one singular term). By the equivalence mentioned two sentences back, (5) yields

(6) P is possessed by s;
      So, s has being.

Now, the contraposition of premise and conclusion, (6) yields

(7) s does not have being;
      So, P is not possessed by s.

Since P is an arbitrary property, we obtain

(8) s does not have being;
      So, nothing is possessed by s.

Notice that the principle of independence, the dictum that
(9) $(EP)P$ is possessed by s;
      So, s has being

is invalid, is (as noted in the previous chapter) equivalent to the dictum that

(10) *s* does not have being;
      So, nothing is possessed by *s*

is invalid. The invalidity of (10) is a close formal paraphrase of Meinong's remark that the nonbeing (*Nichtsein*) of an object does not 'affect' its having a nature (*Sosein*), and contradicts the traditional acknowledgment of the validity of (8). So it follows that the principle of independence implies the invalidity of (8), hence of its genesis (5), and thus of the traditional constraint that the singular term of the simplest kind of predication must refer to a subsistent. Clearly, the argument can be generalized to a predication with *n* singular terms. So the principle of independence does indeed entail the denial of the traditional constraint.

The relationship between the principle of independence and the denial of the traditional constraint also holds in the opposite direction. That is, the denial of the traditional constraint entails the principle of independence. The argument, again, is indirect, and is confined to the simplest case.

Suppose, then, for indirect proof that

(11) *Gs*;
      So, *s* has being

is invalid, but

(12) (E*P*)*P* is possessed by *s*;
      So, *s* has being

is valid. Now assume a predication

(13) *Gs*.

Then, by the equivalence principle employed in the previous argument, it follows that

(14) *P* is possessed by *s*.

Existential generalization on (14) yields

(15) $(EP)P$ is possessed by s.

But, by the hypothesis of indirect proof, (15) entails

(16) s has being.

Hence,

(17) Gs;
So, s has being

is valid, contradicting the hypothesis for indirect proof. The argument can also easily be generalized to a predication of n singular terms. Combining this result with the earlier one yields the conclusion that the principle of independence is equivalent to rejection of the traditional constraint, the constraint that the purported referents of each of the singular terms in a predication has being.

There is an important proviso to the above reasoning, best brought out by example. The symbolism described in note 2 (p. 42) will be helpful. There, a (1-place) general term was depicted as an expression of the form

(18) $(\dot{x})(Fx)$,

where the dot is an operator producing general terms out of open sentences,

(19) Fx,

for instance. To illustrate, '$\dot{x}$' when applied to the open sentence

(20) x is spherical

yields the general term

(21) $(\dot{x})(x$ is spherical$)$.

With this notation at hand we can now express an important logical principle, a kind of abstraction principle:

A $(\dot{x})(Fx)s$ if and only if Fs

This might be read:

> *s* is a thing which is *F* (say, spherical)
> if and only if *s* is *F*.

Now for the example.

Suppose a predication is complex; that is, suppose the general term in the predication contains a logical operator – specifically, the truth-functional conjunction 'and'. In particular, suppose the predication is

(22) The spheroid which is such that it is not a spheroid is spherical and is such that it is not a spheroid.

This statement contains the complex general term

(23) spherical and is such that it is not a spheroid.

Applying A to (22) yields

(24) The spheroid which is such that it is not a spheroid is spherical and it is not the case that the spheroid which is such that it is not a spheroid is spherical,

a conjunction of a predication and its negation, and hence a contradiction. In classical statement logic a contradiction implies anything. Hence (24) and (22), by virtue of A, imply

(25) The spheroid which is such that it is not a spheroid has being, and thus we have a counterexample to claim that an argument of the form

(26) *Gs*;
So, *s* has being

is invalid. For (22) is a predication and implies (25), a conclusion of the form

(27) *s* has being.

The proviso, then, in the reasoning to show that the principle of independence is equivalent to denial of the classical constraint is that A, the principle of abstraction, does not hold.

But what independent reason is there to think that A, a principle which will appear again at the end of this chapter, is false?

In the past decade and a half evidence has mounted that the principle of abstraction, in its present form, is unacceptable. I will mention just two sources here. A study by Ronald Scales, on the one hand, and an essay by Robert Stalnaker and Richmond Thomason, on the other hand, can be interpreted as providing evidence that A is false.[12] (The version of abstraction in Scales' study is expressed in terms of an operator that generates singular terms, rather than general terms, out of open sentences. But that difference is, in my opinion, not essential to the point being made here.)

Consider the following instance of A:

> (28) $(\dot{x})$ (it is not the case that x has being) Vulcan if and only if it is not the case that Vulcan has being.

According to Scales, the left-hand side 'attributes the property' of nonbeing to Vulcan and is false because 'nothing has no properties'. On the other hand the right hand side denies that Vulcan has 'the property of' being, and is true. So, for Scales, A is disconfirmed.

Consider next the following instance of A:

> (29) $(\dot{x})$ (Necessarily x is a citizen), the president of the United States if and only if necessarily the president of the United States is a citizen.

According to Stalnaker and Thomason, the left-hand side of (29) attributes a necessary property to the President of the United States. That is, it says: the president of the United States is necessarily a citizen. But this quite likely is false. However, the right-hand side, which says that necessarily the president of the United States has the property of being a citizen, is surely true. So again A is disconfirmed.

---

[12] Ronald Scales, *Attribution and Existence*, University of Michigan Microfilms (1969); and Robert Stalnaker and Richmond Thomason, 'Attribution in First-Order Modal Logic', *Theoria*, 3 (1968), pp. 203–7.

The above instances of A involve complex general terms, general terms involving at least one logical operator, negation in the first disconfirmation instance and necessity in the second disconfirmation instance. If the general term is simple – contains no logical operator – A seems to portend no untoward consequences.

It might be thought that there is another threat to the assertion that an argument of the form

(30) Gs;
      So, s has being

is invalid. Thus let 'G' be 'being'. The result is surely valid, and cannot be averted by appeal to the failure of abstraction because 'being' is a simple general term. Not true. As will emerge in Chapter 6.

(31) being

can be construed as shorthand for

(32) $(\dot{x})(Ey)(y = x)$.

This is a complex general term and reads

(33) Thing which is such that there subsists something the same as it.

So the remarks about abstraction here apply also, and the potential threat is averted.

What exactly does rejection of the traditional constraint amount to? The dictum that the constituent singular terms $s_1 \ldots s_n$ of a predication need not refer to subsistents has two quite distinct options *vis à vis* the traditional constraint. One option is that the singular terms in the predication may be irreferential, that is, may have no referents of any kind, subsistent or nonsubsistent. The other option is that the singular terms in the predication though perhaps not referring to any subsistent object may yet refer to nonsubsistent objects. Such is the ambiguity in the phrase 'the singular term s does not refer to a subsistent'. So the important point emerges that the principle

of independence does not by itself imply that there are nonsubsistent objects. That the argument from

> The round square is self-identical

to

> the round square subsists

is invalid does not itself imply that 'the round square' refers to
a nonsubsistent. Of course, Meinong believed the round
square to be an object, but, to say it once more, this belief is not
sustained by the principle of independence *alone*.[13]

Of the two options about the reference of singular terms,
Meinong's view is the second; it follows from the principle of
independence and the core principle CT because CT requires
every singular term in a predication to *specify an object*. So the
possibility that the round square, for example, is not an object
at all is ruled out, and the expression 'the round square' thus
refers to a nonsubsistent object. At its core, then, Meinong's
theory of predication differs from the traditional theory in
'substance' but not in principle.

What then of the principle of noncontradiction? For, as
noted in the previous section, a reason for adopting the traditional constraint, given both the traditional theory of
predication and the 'natural' designation principle that the
designation of an expression of the form 'the so and so' must be
a thing of which the basis of that expression ('so and so' in 'the
so and so') is true, 'givens' evidently accepted by Meinong, is
that the law of noncontradiction is violated – or so Russell
seems to have believed. Just as the free logician rejects the
logical principle of specification in the wake of the decision to
tolerate singular terms that do not refer to subsistents, so an

---

[13] To be sure Meinong sometimes seems to have expressed the principle of independence so as to involve direct commitment to nonsubsistent objects. Witness his
'paradoxical' way of putting it (cf. the previous chapter); there are objects such that
there are no such objects. Nevertheless, the full account of that principle in 'On the
Theory of Objects' supports, I believe, the view taken above that the principle of
independence does not commit one to nonsubsistent objects. Meinong's 'paradoxical' expression is really a natural consequence of that principle in conjunction with
other principles, in particular, his theory of predication.

intellectually fearless Meinong, refusing to cavil before the logically 'unthinkable', restricts the law of noncontradiction to subsistent objects.[14] Russell, as noted earlier, protested loudly about the extremism of Meinong's way out. He accused Meinong of misunderstanding the range of the principle of noncontradiction: it applies, he said to propositions (or objectives), not to objects – a mystifying complaint from the man who said that nonsubsistent '*objects* . . . are apt to infringe the law of [non]contradiction.'[15] Even ignoring Russell's hypocrisy, his complaint is unacceptable. It is as unconvincing as the complaint that the widely acknowledged restriction on specification to the objects that subsist reflects a misconception of the range of specification (classically construed) because it really applies only to statements (or propositions); for that principle declares that every statement (or proposition) of the form '$Fs \supset (Ex)(Fx)$' is true, where 'F' is a statement containing 's', and 'x' replaces 's' in 'Fx'. But, in

---

[14] Actually, in print he restricts the principle to possible objects, but some possibles are nonsubsistent – for example, Pegasus. Apparently the reason he did not include refractory cases like the king of the United States, an example thought to frustrate the law of noncontradiction, is his distinction between nuclear and extranuclear properties. Thus the first occurrence of 'existent' in 'The existent king of the United States is not an existent king of the United States' is nuclear (a 'watered down' sense of 'existent'), but the second occurrence could be extranuclear. If it is extranuclear, the statement in question is not of the form 'The so and so is not a so and so' and hence violation of noncontradiction is avoided. On the other hand, if the second occurrence of 'existent' is nuclear, the statement in question is simply false – and again contradiction is avoided. Still, in the absence of a theory about the exact relationship between objects and extranuclear properties, it is hard to see how this distinction really helps Meinong after all. For what blocks the possibility that 'existent' in both occurrences of the word in the statement 'The existent king of the United States is not an existent king of the United States' is extranuclear? If nothing does, then contradiction threatens again because the statement in question has the form 'The so and so is not a so and so' and would seem to be true. Indeed, the doctrine of nuclear and extranuclear properties is a difficult one, not least because of the lack of a clear standard for telling which is which. For example, apparently some of the Master's disciples interpreted Meinong to hold that 'existent' and its synonyms stand for a '*Sosein*', that is, a nuclear property, *contra* Findlay's interpretation in *Meinong's Theory of Objects and Values*. See, for example, the essay by Ameseder in A. Meinong (ed.), *Untersuchungen zur Gegenstandstheorie und Psychologie*, p. 79. Note, however, Terence Parsons' *Nonexistent Objects* for likely protest to the contrary. Caution thus seems to dictate a wider restriction than Meinong first proposed, that is, the restriction must be extended to exclude all nonsubsistent objects.

[15] 'On Denoting', p. 45; my italics.

Russell's words, this conclusion 'is intolerable'.

In the foregoing discussion, the principle of noncontradiction has been construed as the principle that no statement of the form 'A and not A' is true, a construal that indeed conforms with the language of the debate between Meinong and Russell. Some, agreeing with Russell's sentiment though deploring his inconsistent attitude toward the scope of the principle of noncontradiction, may still plead that Meinong's rejection of the unlimited principle of noncontradiction is far less plausible than the free logician's rejection of the unlimited principle of specification on the ground that the former is a 'basic law of thought' but the latter is not. Even presuming such an objection not to rest on confusing the present principle with another which often goes by the same name – the principle that no statement can be both true and false – or on the patently sophistical assertion that rejection of unlimited noncontradiction presupposes its acceptance, still it is difficult to see what credence to attach to the objection. From the point of view of pure logic all logical principles are on the same footing *vis à vis* the laws of thought.

One cannot be indifferent, however, to the effects of Meinong's embracing restricted noncontradiction on beingless objects – or at the very least on the 'world' of impossible nonsubsistents. Nor can John Findlay's sympathetic apology below entirely mitigate the feeling of strain that must arise, even in the fibers of the most ardent of Meinong's disciples, from the forced acknowledgment that the spheroid which is such that it is not a spheroid is spherical and also is nonspherical.

We speak of the *world* of *Aussersein*, but in reality the objects which have no being do not constitute a world. They are a chaos of incoherent fragments.... From another point of view *Aussersein* is incapable of scientific treatment because of its excessive richness. In the case of the actual world we can always ask whether a certain object is comprised in it or not; the question is interesting, because some things are excluded from it. The realm of *Aussersein*, however, has no such exclusiveness; every possibility or impossibility is comprised in it, and this fact silences a multitude of questions.[16]

In the end the question must be faced: if 'possession of contradictory properties' is not evidence against the objecthood of a declared candidate for that office, what can be? Or, by virtue of semantic ascent, the question that must be faced is this: if contradiction is not evidence of falsehood, then what incontrovertibly could be? One is forced to agree after all with the conviction that the free logician's restriction on specification *is* in a different category of plausibility from Meinong's restriction on noncontradiction (though not, of course, with the reason just adduced for that conviction).

Avoidance of conflict with the principle of noncontradiction has been a dominating theme in recent attempts to develop theories of nonexistent objects in the manner of Meinong, or at least approaches inspired by his theory of objects. The various strategies are occasioned by differing decisions about the amount and character of *Aussersein* that ought to be preserved, decisions that bear on one or another (or combinations) of the three basic beliefs alleged to have produced the trouble in the first place: (1) the core of the traditional theory of predication, (2) that 'so and so' is true of the designatum of 'the so and so', and (3) that every singular term refers.

Suppose one is willing to tolerate all of *Aussersein*, but is prepared to give up any difference between the nonsubsistents. This means abandoning (2) – as free logicians know. This attitude, reminiscent of Frege, is effected by selecting a single nonsubsistent as referent for all singular terms not referring to subsistents.[17] Though preserving conviction (1) and (3), this stratagem does violence to serious efforts to produce a theory of nonsubsistent *objects*, a major standard of adequacy being the preservation of *differences* between the spheroid which is such that it is not a spheroid and Pegasus, and perhaps also

[16] *Meinong's Theory of Objects and Values* (2nd edn), pp. 56–7. Findlay himself cannot stand the strain which acknowledgment of nonsubsistents with 'contradictory properties' induces: see his remarks on page 341 of the same book.

[17] See, for example, Dana Scott's treatment, 'Existence and Description in Formal Logic'.

between the spheroid which is such that it is not a spheroid and the decision procedure for quantification theory. Thus, the present approach is not seriously entertained by those seriously interested in Meinong's project.

Some seek to eliminate certain beingless objects in order to save the rest along with their various differences from other of their more well-behaved compatriots. Terence Parsons, in his book *Nonexistent Objects*, espouses this sort of position denying objecthood to the spheroid which is such that it is not a spheroid (but not to the round square), thus rejecting (3). A full-blown theory of nuclear and extranuclear properties is introduced to prevent the existent king of the United States from initiating contradictions, a right surely not divine even for him. This course has here the non-Meinongian result that the statement 'The spheroid which is such that it is not a spheroid is spherical' is not a predication, at least as Meinong's theory of predication has been rendered here.

Some seek to preserve the richness of the world of *Aussersein* in ways that lead directly to an amendment or abandonment of CT. William Rapaport, for instance, believes that the character of *Aussersein* demands two distinct varieties of predication but not abandonment of (2) and (3), if I understand him correctly. Details of his multipredicational approach, and how it avoids conflict with the law of noncontradiction, may be found in his essay 'Meinongian Theories and a Russellian Paradox'.[18]

Finally there are some others, the Routleys for two,[19] if the ensuing semantic extrapolation of their views is just, who both insist on the full range and variety of beingless objects *and* on the principles (1), (2) and (3). What is abandoned in this case, interestingly, is the abstraction principle. To explain the Routleys' approach best, some of the symbolism described in note 2 of this chapter (p. 42) will be helpful.

With this notation one can express CT much more rigor-

---

[18] See pp. 153–80.
[19] See Richard Routley, *Exploring Meinong's Jungle*, Monograph No. 3, Philosophy Department, Australian National University, Canberra 1980.

ously and briefly. Consider, for example, the simplest case where the general term is a 1-place general term – say, '$(\dot{x})(x$ is spherical)' – and the singular term is 'The spheroid which is such that it is not a spheroid'. Then we have the following special instance of CT:

> '$(\dot{x})$ (x is spherical), the spheroid which is such that it is not a spheroid' is true (or false) according as '$(\dot{x})$ (x is spherical)' is true (or false) of the spheroid which is such that it is not a spheroid.

Now, in the Routleys' view, because CT holds, and because also 'The spheroid which is such that it is not a spheroid' has a referent and both '$(\dot{x})$ (x is spherical)' and '$(\dot{x})$ (x is not spherical)' are true of that referent, it follows that both

> (i) $(\dot{x})$ (x is spherical), the spheroid which is such that it is not a spheroid

and

> (ii) $(\dot{x})$ (x is not spherical), the spheroid which is such that it is not a spheroid

are both true. But no contradiction results unless the abstraction principle

> A $(\dot{x})(Fx)t$ if and only if Ft

is adopted. For only with A can one get to

> (iii) The spheroid which is such that it is not a spheroid is spherical

and

> (iv) The spheroid which is such that it is not a spheroid is not spherical

from (i) and (ii). But A is precisely what the Routleys reject. Probably this approach meshes best with Meinong's goals. For if the earlier argument about the equivalence of the principle of independence and the traditional constraint is correct, then it follows that the principle of abstraction – at least for complex general terms – must be rejected by Meinong, though there is no evidence that he was ever aware of the problem. This consideration tends to support the Routleys' course of action. It also means that the widely held conviction that the set of Meinongian beliefs expressed by (1)–(3) above violates the law of noncontradiction is fundamentally unsound, Russell's argument to the contrary notwithstanding. That conviction depends on the viability of the principle of abstraction.

The value of the Routleys' approach, nevertheless, is essentially critical, for the fact remains that their treatment is still more of a program than a developed theory. Very little, for example, is said by the Routleys about the conditions under which a general term is true of an object – or at least the equivalent of that relation. Nor is it always clear whether and how nonbeings are distinguished; is, for example, the impossible object referred to by 'the spheroid which is such that it is not a spheroid' the same as (or different from) the impossible object referred to by 'Heimdal' (the man born simultaneously of nine sibling jotun maidens), let alone the same as (or different from) the impossible object referred to by 'the decision procedure for first order predicate logic'? The answer is not forthcoming in the Routleys' discussion.

Much of the Routleys' effort seems directed at poking holes in the arguments of others who believe Meinong's theoretical pronouncements outrageous and/or simply wrong. It is certainly true that the abstraction principle discussed above is a major source of vulnerability in most arguments about the faulty logical character of Meinong's theory of objects. But this does not absolve the defender of Meinong from the positive responsiblity of producing a workable account of Meinong's theory. A positive account of Meinong's theory is especially important because, to my knowledge, all attempts to produce such an account have resulted in a significant departure from Meinong's theory if the account is consistent.[20]

[20] However, just such an account, although very rudimentary, is being attempted in a

The constituency of *Aussersein* is something even Meinong worried about. He talked now and then about 'defective objects', the designators of which could only be taken to refer to objects in the most strained and tenuous sense, if at all.[21] That 'the thought which is about a thought which is not about itself' does not designate an object can, of course, be made compatible with the principle that every singular term refers by denying termhood to the expression in question – for example, on type-theoretical grounds. But such a course is not open in the case of recalcitrant examples such as the spheroid which is such that it is not a spheroid, whose definite description is type-theoretically proper. It is this kind of case which tends to bring about the abandonment of the collection of beliefs (1)–(3) as a whole, and thus directly affects either Meinong's theory of predication or what is to be considered a legitimate instance of the logical form of predication.

There is another feature of Meinong's conception of predication which bears discussion no matter what the ultimate constituency of *Aussersein* is; all that is required is that there be at least one nonsubsistent. His conception – which is just the traditional theory unconstrained – is *distensional*.[22] The property is worth talking about for at least two reasons: first, it has an indirect effect in illuminating Findlay's counterposition of Meinongian logic to what he calls 'extensional logic',[23] and second, its relation *vis à vis* the principle of extensionality, a principle much discussed from Frege through Quine.

What is the distension of a (general) term? It is the set of *all* objects the term is true of. The distension of 'man' is the set of *all* objects – subsistent (Meinong) and nonsubsistent (Ichabod

forthcoming essay on Meinong's theory of meaning by Peter Simons and Edgar Morscher of the University of Salzburg. Their intention is to present an account that violates no basic Meinongian dicta including the three at the beginning of the next chapter.

[21] Meinong, *On Emotional Presentation.*

[22] See Parsons, *Nonexistent Objects*, p. 75.

[23] *Meinong's Theory of Objects and Values*, p. 339. Here, Findlay writes: 'Meinong in his doctrine of *Aussersein* has performed an act of incomparable merit, he has prevented the realistic, first order interests dominant in science and extensional logic from misrepresenting the higher-order structures of experience...'

Crane), possible (Meinong, Ichabod Crane) and impossible (the spheroid which is such that it is not a spheroid) – that general term is true of. It is to be distinguished from the *extension* and *comprehension* of a general term, familiar from the traditional logic of terms, and carefully delineated in C. I. Lewis' famous essay, 'The Modes of Meaning'.[24] Lewis says essentially that the extension of a general term is the set of subsistent objects that term is true of, and its comprehension is the set of possible objects that term is true of. So the comprehension of a term includes its extension, and perhaps also some nonsubsistent objects (for example, Ichabod Crane). In the same vein, the distension includes its comprehension, and thence its extension, and yet more objects – for example, the impossible nonsubsistent Heimdal. There are terms with empty extensions, for example, 'winged horse', with empty comprehensions, for example, 'round square', and depending on the final resolution of 'defective objects' perhaps even with empty distensions, for example, 'thought about a thought not about itself'.

Contemporary talk about extensionality has somewhat distorted the traditional notion. For example, the extension of the general term, in the contemporary parlance originating in Carnap's classic *Meaning and Necessity*, say, 'winged horse', is customarily taken to be simply the set of objects it is true of, as opposed to the intension of that term (a property, a function, etc.). So construed it would comprise, for instance, merely possible objects (such as Pegasus) as well as actual objects (such as Meinong). It is not surprising, therefore, that traditional and current talk of extensions can yield different verdicts about whether a given theory of predication violates the principle of extensionality, a principle which demands that coextensional general terms be everywhere substitutable *salva veritate*. Suppose, for example, that the ontology of a given language contains at least one nonsubsistent, and that it is taken to be the referent of all singular terms not having subsistents as bearers. Then, according to the traditional view about extensions, the theory of predication in that language might prove to be nonextensional, but not so in more contemporary talk of extensions – via the same kind of proof anyway. Thus, traditionally speaking, 'winged horse' and 'subsistent winged horse' have the same extension, namely, the null set, because there are no subsistent winged horses; but whereas the predication 'Pegasus is a winged horse' could be true, the predication 'Pegasus is a subsistent winged horse' would surely be false. In contrast, contemporary talk of extensions would eschew this proof of nonextensionality simply by denying the coextensionality of 'winged horse' and 'subsistent winged horse', the former having at least one member in its extension, in the requisite sense of 'extension', and the latter having a null extension in that same sense of 'extension'. The upshot of this discussion is that, traditionally, to specify the extension of a (general) term requires more than specifying a certain extensional entity, a set; it requires that attention be paid to the ontic character of the members of that set – that the objects all be subsistent (= existent in Quine's terms). And the same applies to the notions of comprehension and distension – which indeed have not received a proper treatment in contemporary talk of extension and intension.[25] But it is precisely these distinctions that are important to an understanding of Findlay's preference for Meinong's logic over 'extensional logic'. For in the contemporary mode, Meinong's logic may be every bit as extensional as 'extensional logic'; in the traditional mode, it certainly is not, as the argument above shows. So Findlay's preference for Meinongian logic – however that logic may be spelled out in detail – over 'extensional logic' can be properly evaluated only after being translated into the traditional mode.

A similar point can be made about the famous analytic principle of Frege's that the extension of a complex is a function of the extensions of its parts. Whether or not the Meinongian theory of predication violates this principle depends entirely

---

[25] Not surprisingly because of the (until recently) general aversion to nonsubsistent objects sponsored by the major analytic philosophers from Russell to Quine.

on whether 'extension' is construed traditionally or contemporarily. Construed in the latter way it may not fail in the Meinongian theory of predication, but construed traditionally it certainly does; for in the latter sense of 'extensional', the truth value of the predication 'Heimdal is impossible' (as his mothers knew) is not dependent solely on the extensions of the appropriate terms in this statement but requires appeal also to distensions – for example, to the distension of the general term 'impossible'.

4

INDEPENDENCE AND PREDICATION: II

I. A NONTRADITIONAL THEORY OF PREDICATION

For the Meinongian the previous chapter began promisingly enough, but ended in considerable philosophical uncertainty. The general if mistaken reaction was that the three Meinongian (or Meinong-like) convictions

(i) All singular terms (including 'The spheroid which is such that it is not a spheroid') refer;

(ii) A statement is a predication just in case it results from joining general term to singular terms and is true (or false) according as the n-place general term is true (or false) of the n-tuple of things specified by the several singular terms;

(iii) The general term comprising the basis of a definite description ('spheroid which is such that it is not a spheroid' in 'The spheroid which is such that it is not a spheroid', for instance) is true of the referent of that definite description

cannot jointly be sustained. The serious options contemplated were an *Aussersein* depleted of the spheroid which is such that it is not a spheroid (and the like), and hence rejection of the singular term 'The spheroid which is such that it is not a spheroid' (and the like) as referential, or abandonment of CT. But, the viability of the principle of abstraction aside, this way of presenting the options is still misleading, because it suggests that the way to save the core of the Meinongian theory of predication is simply to abandon such things as the spheroid which is such that it is not a spheroid (or, in virtue of semantic ascent, to abandon the conviction that the singular term 'The spheroid which is such that it is not a spheroid' is referential). But dropping 'The spheroid which is such that it is not a spheroid' from the ranks of referential singular terms only has the desired effect in a depleted set of Meinongian philosophical convictions about logical form. Thus, suppose one were also consumed by the conviction, held strongly by Meinong, that the statements

(1) That is spherical,

where 'that' specifies a golf ball in the visual field of speaker and hearer, and

(2) The spheroid which is such that it is not a spheroid is spherical

have the same logical form. Since (1) is undeniably a predication in everyone's theory, so is (2). However, since, by agreement, 'The spheroid which is such that it is not a spheroid' is irreferential, there is no thing it specifies for the general term to be true (or false) of. Hence, by CT, (2) cannot be a predication after all. The upshot is that belief in the predicational form of (1), and belief in the sameness of the logical form of (1) and (2), lays a heavy burden on CT. In fact, it must fail in the face of these additional assumptions. Meinong-inspired philosophers who accept the Russellian aversion to the philosophically unwholesome character of at least the spheroid which is such that it is not a spheroid are, given strong Meinongian convictions, faced after all with contemplating another core principle of predication.

Actually there is a wide-ranging interest in exploring an alternative to CT. First, there are free logicians who, believing there to be no objects but the beingful ones, accept the above convictions concerning the logical form of (1) and (2) while eschewing, of course, the referential character not only of 'The spheroid which is such that it is not a spheroid' but also of

'Pegasus' (*contra* Meinong or Neo-Meinongians).[1] Second, even Meinong-inspired philosophers, who deny that everything is an object, yet who nevertheless insist on the predicational character of simple statements containing genuinely irreferential singular terms, need an alternative to CT.[2] Third, and

---

[1] A good example is provided by Tyler Burge, in a recent debate with Richard Grandy over the correct formulation of free logic: R. Grandy, 'Predication and Singular Terms', *Noûs*, 11 (1977), pp.163–7; T. Burge, 'Truth and Singular Terms', *Noûs*, 8 (1974), pp. 309–25). Both of them hold statements such as (1) and (2) to be predications, but they disagree on the truth-value attaching to statements such as

> (3) The present king of France is the present king of France,

Grandy holding it to be true, and Burge false. Grandy puts the matter this way:

> This makes it appear that we have formalized different concepts of identity and disagree about the correct formulation of the identity sense of 'is' in English, but in fact the dispute is more general and does not turn on questions of interpreting identity. The more general difference is that where F is any atomic predicate and *t* is any nondenoting term, Burge thinks that F*t* is false, whereas I think that at least some instances are true ... the difference between us is a matter of interpreting predication – that Burge's predication has exisential import whereas mine is neutral.

The context of Grandy's remarks makes it clear that he is thinking of the predications as simply the set of atomic sentences, and the issue between himself and Burge as one concerning the proper truth-values of predications with nondenoting terms. Grandy thinks their disagreement reflects a difference in 'concepts of predication'. Indeed, in terms of the discussion of predication in the last chapter, different concepts of predication are being offered by Grandy and Burge, Grandy's concept being quite traditional at the core, but Burge's quite untraditional, despite his agreement with the Russellian position on the truth-values of statements containing at least one expression not referring to an actual object. In fact, he says explicitly (in the essay cited above) that his disagreement with Russell concerns the logical form of statements such as (2) above, Russell denying that they are predications, and Burge believing that they are. To emphasize one of the main points of the last chapter, Burge and Russell have different views about the predicational status of (2), because even though they share the same constraint on predication, their *ways of computing* the truth-value of (2) are different though the end result, falsehood, is the same. Grandy, on the other hand, evaluates statements like (2) much as Meinong does – he has an outer domain of nonexistent objects, one of which is the value of 'The spheroid which is such that it is not a spheroid', a core theory of predication like Russell's, but he rejects the constraint that if a statement is a predication, its singular terms must refer to actual objects.

[2] A case in point may be Terence Parsons' treatment in his provocative book *Nonexistent Objects*. There, the singular term 'The round square' is a referential singular term. But the singular term 'The thing that is round and it is not the case that it is round' is not referential. Yet, apparently, the statement 'The thing that is round and it is not the case that it is round is round' has the same logical form as 'The round square is round'. So given the predicational character of the latter statement, however that would be spelled out by Parsons, the former statement must be predicational. And this sense of predication would be quite different than in a theory

finally, there is a vaguely-felt discontent with the core of the traditional theory, CT, at least among many non-Meinongians. It might be put this way. Ideally the logical form of a statement should not depend on *facts* about reference. CT violates this ideal because the mere fact that the singular term 'Vulcan' in

(4) Vulcan (i.e., the nonexistent planet) rotates

does not refer is enough to disqualify (4) as predicational. Why? Because the truth-value of (4), if any at all, cannot be assessed by means of what the general term 'rotates' is true (or false) of, there being no Vulcan. No doubt it is such a primordial intuition that drove many to the Russellian extreme of denying that (4) is predicational just because 'Vulcan' is not a referring kind of expression at all.

Now that the issue is joined, it will be valuable to consider a pair of alternatives that are not acceptable for one reason or another. One alternative involves appeal not only to the referents of terms but also to their 'senses'. If, in the manner of Carnap's *Meaning and Necessity*, the senses of general terms are thought of as attributes, and the senses of singular terms are thought of as individual concepts, then an alternative core principle of predication might be expressed as follows: A statement has the logical form of a predication just in case it joins general term to singular terms such that the result is true or false according as the n-tuple of individual concepts associated with the singular terms is subsumed under the attribute associated with the general term. The notion of subsumption in this conception of predication, a conception reminiscent of Aldo Bressan in his remarkable treatise on modal logic,[3] need not be more fully explained to see that this nontraditional conception of predication would be unacceptable to Meinongians and most extensionally inclined non-Meinongians. Meinong, like most ontologists of an extensionalist bent, rejects senses. A

where the singular term 'The thing that is round but it is not the case that it is round' is treated as referential.

[3] *A General Interpreted Modal Calculus*, Yale University Press, New Haven, 1973.

theory of predication appealing to senses is for all of them definitely beyond the pale. And this is so despite the promise of accommodating the predicational character of both (1) and (2); it suffices to note that the roadblock of no referent in the case of (2) is successfully skirted by the individual concept of the spheroid which is such that it is not a spheroid, and that the notion of subsumption can be so construed that it applies both to empty and nonempty concepts.

How about Meinong's notion of an incomplete object? Might not an alternative to CT which appeals to such objects be promising? If so, what would it look like? The alternative being contemplated conceivably might be put in at least two ways. The first is simply to add to CT the specific phrase 'the incomplete object referred to by the singular term t'; the second is to construe a statement of the form 'the general term is true (or false) of the n-tuple of objects specified by the singular terms' in CT to be true just in case the n-tuple of incomplete objects associated with the singular terms has (or has not) 'involved' or 'embedded'[4] in it the incomplete object associated with the general term.

The first formulation will not do because it applies only to statements in which reference is made to an incomplete object, leaving the whole domain of statements about complete objects untreated. So the second formulation is, on the face of it, more promising when incomplete objects are employed; that a singular term may have associated with it an incomplete object which 'determines' the reference of that singular term is, indeed, in one commentator's view, good Meinongian doctrine. If so, a statement – for instance, 'The golf ball is spherical' – can be about a complete object while having its logical form expressed in terms of incomplete objects. The authority in question is John Findlay. Speaking of a particular kind of incomplete object called an auxiliary object and its relation to what is called the ultimate object, Findlay writes:

---

[4] 'Embedded' (*implektiert*) is an expression used by Meinong. See the passage from Findlay quoted below.

Hence we may call the indeterminate square thing which the content *could* present an *auxiliary object* (*Hilfsgegenstand*), and the determinate square thing which the content *does* present the *ultimate object* (*Zielgegenstand*). Adopting this frankly fictitious mode of speaking, we may say that, where the ultimate object of our reference is a concrete existent or one of its aspects, we refer to it by means of an indeterminate auxiliary object. It is through one or other of the incomplete objects embedded in it that a complete object is given to our thought. It is by means of the incomplete object 'man' that the son of Callias, who is more than merely a man, is given to us. We think of a certain concrete object as 'a table', or 'a piece of furniture', or 'a brown thing', or 'a hard thing on which we have bruised ourselves in the dark', and so on.[5]

A little later, in a footnote, Findlay makes the provocative remark:

It is perhaps worth observing that Meinong's distinction between the auxiliary and the ultimate object does much the same work as Frege's distinction between *Sinn* (sense) and *Bedeutung* (reference).[6]

The second formulation of the core principle of predication via incomplete objects is, indeed, promising at first glance. For like the formulation in terms of individual concepts, it is certainly not implausible that it can accommodate statements such as

> The spheroid which is such that it is not a spheroid is a thing which is spherical

containing the irreferential singular term 'The spheroid which is such that it is not a spheroid'. This presumes, of course, some reasonable explanation of the relation of embeddedness. Unlike the formulation in terms of individual concepts, it appeals only to genuine 'objects'; the incomplete object which is a horse *is* a horse but the individual concept of a horse is not a horse. But ultimately this alternative formulation of the logical form of predication in terms of incomplete objects will not work. In the first place it is not clear how it can avoid the

---

[5] *Meinong's Theory of Objects and Values* (2nd edn), p. 177.
[6] *Ibid.*, p. 184.

contradiction between (2) and

> (5) The spheroid which is such that it is not a spheroid is a thing which is not spherical.

For (5) seems quite as acceptable as a predication as (2), and surely the incomplete object associated with the general term 'thing which is not spherical' is embedded in the incomplete object which is the spheroid which is such that it is not a spheroid under any reasonable understanding of the concept of embeddedness. In the second place it is just not clear how the theory applies to statements like

> That is spherical.

This statement, which surely would be counted a predication, makes reference – given the earlier context – to a complete object. But it is not at all clear what incomplete object expressed by 'That' is operative in determining the truth-value of that statement, if any.

Finally, there is the complaint that the current theory of predication, as well as that in terms of individual concepts, promotes an illusion, the illusion that the relationship between logical form and evaluation rules is as direct as Kaplan's theory has it, and as has been assumed in previous pages of this essay. This objection bears extended discussion, and that will be one of the principal themes of the rest of this chapter.

The question needs to be kept in mind whether the adoption of a nontraditional core principle of predication requires rejection of Meinong's principle of independence. The answer is no, as indeed was asserted in the last chapter. When attention is restricted to the unacceptable core principle of predication just canvassed, the answer is pretty clearly no. There certainly is no inextricable connection between the principle of independence and these faulted theories. Consider just the theory appealing to senses. It needs no lengthy argument to see that the principle of independence is compatible with the core principle of predication appealing to senses; that

The winged horse is winged

can be a true predication in virtue of the attribute of being winged subsuming the concept of the winged horse, yet that there be no winged horse, seems straightforward enough. And the extension to the core principle of predication couched in terms of incomplete objects in the same spirit seems easy.

These core principles, however, are not the focus of consideration in the rest of this chapter. Nevertheless the answer to the question: Does adoption of a nontraditional core principle of predication require rejection of Meinong's principle of independence? is still no; as will soon be clear, the nontraditional core principle to be outlined below not only has exponents who adopt the principle of independence but also those who reject it. The decision to regard the principle of independence as the lifting of a constraint on the core of the traditional theory of predication relied in part on just this fact.

II. PREDICATION AND TRUTH-VALUE

Philosophers disagree passionately on the truth-value of statements such as

(2) The spheroid which is such that it is not a spheroid is spherical,

and even about statements such as

(6) The spheroid which is such that it is not a spheroid is the spheroid which is such that it is not a spheroid.

Some, like Meinong, say they are both true, some say they are both false, and some even say they are both truth-valueless. Moreover, there are opinions that differentiate between (2) and (6); for example, some hold (6) true (by logic alone) and (2) truth-valueless. In general, the problem is how to devise a consistent and plausible treatment of statements containing irreferential singular terms, however one draws the barriers around that class of expressions. There are, of course, limits on which treatments can qualify as worthy candidates. For example, any treatment that counted

> (7) The spheroid which is such that it is not a spheroid exists

as true would be unacceptable. Virtually every philosopher, including Meinong, regards (7) as false, and with good reason. (Here 'exists' is the mundane use, and not the special use of that word explained above in the Introduction, which some attribute to Quine. According to that usage, since Meinong believes there is an object that is the spheroid which is such that it is not a spheroid, he believes that the spheroid which is such that it is not a spheroid exists, and hence that (7) is true.)

The immediate point to be made in this section is that the truth-value one finally fixes on for statements such as (2) and (6) may have little or nothing to do with one's belief that both are predications; the decision about what truth-value, if any, a statement actually has can remain unclear despite one's knowing, or believing, that a given statement has the logical form of a predication. This fact requires a reassessment of the idea that logical form is associated with the way in which a statement is to be evaluated for truth-value.

Consider, for instance, the statements (2) and (6). One may know (or simply believe) that the expression 'The spheroid which is such that it is not a spheroid', contained in both (2) and (6), is irreferential, think both statements are predications, but still be undecided about whether both are true, false, or varying in truth-value. Given that there are widely divergent opinions among those who think that statements like (2) and (6) are predications about what truth-value, if any, each is to be assigned, and how to make that assignment, the sense of predication common to these nontraditionalists will be truly unconventional in one respect. It is that the logical form of predication cannot be associated with a uniform decision about the truth-value, or manner of deciding on the truth-value, if any, which (2) and (6) and their like have – or if one prefers, the truth-value they have in the actual world.

The modified Meinongian (one who believes that there are beingless objects but not that every singular term is referential), free logicians who believe in irreferential singular terms in the broad sense of 'irreferential' but not that there are any beingless objects, and Quine all take statements including such singular terms to be predications. For each of them (2) and (6) indisputably qualify as predications in this nontraditional sense of predication. This sense of predication is, of course, one which differs from the view of predication held by Russell, Meinong and a reform-minded Frege. For the latter can be construed as requiring all predications to have nothing but referential singular terms *and* the logical form so denominated to be associated with a unique evaluation rule.

Quine? Associated with the likes of modified Meinongians and free logicians? There must be a mistake! But there is not, because in the matter at hand, he *is* indeed to be lumped with them as the evidence from sources such as *Word and Object* will show. But notice, first, that such an association, if such there be (and there is), does not mean that Quine must embrace the beingless,[7] nor that he must tolerate any singular terms at all in his canonical language. The Quine being considered now is that Quine hovering somewhere between the natural language and the regimented language; this Quine, unlike Russell, with whom he is so often incorrectly aligned, (i) recognizes expressions such as 'The spheroid which is such that it is not a spheroid' as genuine singular terms, (ii) takes them to be irreferential unlike Meinong and the reform-minded Frege (and some free logicians), and (iii) regards some statements containing irreferential singular terms as predications. The point

---

[7] Quine's canonical language consists of variables, general terms, truth-functional correctives, and quantifiers, and the ontology of that language consists only of extensional entities like physical objects and sets. There are no constant singular terms in the former nor any beingless objects in the latter. The whole apparatus is less than what is available, but nevertheless is believed to be adequate to the needs of science and philosophy. This sort of regimentation is continuous with the spirit and goal of Frege's construction of a scientific language, though it differs in detail. For example, Frege had singular terms in his canonical language and nonextensional entities in his ontology. Useful regimentation, even if artificial in some respects, is not peculiar to philosophy. It occurs in science with some frequency.

is that views about what singular terms are and which statements have the logical form of predication are no sure sign of
how much or how little is comprised in one's ontology.

'Predication', Quine writes, 'joins a general term and a
singular term to form a sentence that is true or false according
as the general term is true or false of the object, *if any*, to which
the singular term refers.'[8] As mentioned in the last chapter,
this notion of predication qua logical form (or construction) is
extended to singular sentences having n-place simple general
terms such as the 2-place general term 'is faster than', 3-place
general terms such as 'is between' and so on, and to singular
sentences containing complex n-place general terms such as
the complex 2-place general term 'tireless runner' and the 3-
place general term 'between Nurmi and someone else', and so
on.[9] The reason, again, is convenience. Also, the word 'join' in
Quine's statement of predication encompasses both concatenation of general and singular term(s), as in 'Meinong thinks',
and copulative infixing, as in 'Meinong is a thinker'.[10]

The expression 'if any' in Quine's statement of predication
is doubly important. For it is this rider that makes Quine an
exponent of a nontraditional view of predication, a rider that
does not occur in CT. And secondly, it permits both (2),

> The spheroid which is such that it is not a spheroid is
> spherical,

and (4)

> Vulcan rotates,

of this chapter to qualify as predications. Thus it is that Quine
parts company in one way both with his ontological friends
such as Russell, and his ontological foes such as Meinong.

As intimated earlier, the statement of predication above is
one that some modified Meinongians and some free logicians

---

[8] *Word and Object*, p. 196; my italics.
[9] *Ibid.*, pp. 106 and 175.
[10] *Ibid.*, p. 96. Not strange at all since it was from Quine that the same policy in the
previous chapter was borrowed.

could well embrace, but never a Russellian. For example, if one looks at the system of free logic developed by Tyler Burge,[11] there is exact agreement on the truth-values[12] that he and Russell ascribe to statements containing 'irreferential' singular terms, but Russell subscribes rather to CT, which Burge cannot. What is more to the point of the present section is that free logicians such as van Fraassen[13] (who considers (6), 'The spheroid which is such that it is not a spheroid is the spheroid which is such that it is not a spheroid', true and (2) perhaps truth-valueless) and Skyrms[14] who, at some moments, holds both (2) and (6) to be truth-valueless) *and* Burge could all subscribe to Quine's statement of predication, *despite* their different opinions about the truth-values these sentences actually have. Let us agree to designate this core principle of predication, latent in Quine's words, 'C$\overline{\text{T}}$'.

Reflection on Quine's evaluation rule reveals that the truth-value of (2), whatever it may be, cannot be dependent on whether the general term 'spherical' is true (or false) of what is specified by the singular term 'The spheroid which is such that it is not a spheroid', there being no such thing for the general term in question to be true (or false) of. This incompleteness provokes two related questions: Is the determination of predication ultimately syntactical after all (at least where irreferential singular terms appear), a mere joining of irreferential singular term(s) and general term to form a statement? And if not, what nonsyntactical means in Quine's incomplete evaluation rule explain why (2) is a predication? For since no way of evaluating statements like (2) is provided, it appears that what is given is purely syntactical.

The incompleteness in Quine's statement of predication

[11] Which in some ways, especially as regards the truth-values of statements containing 'irreferential' singular terms, duplicates the earlier work of Rolf Schock (*Logics Without Existence Assumptions*, Almqvist and Wiksell, Stockholm, 1968) and Ronald Scales (*Attribution and Existence*, University of Michigan Microfilms, 1969). Burge's system is in his paper 'Truth and Singular Terms'.

[12] Or could be if Russellian scope indicators were introduced into Burge's treatment, as Scales showed; see note 11, above.

[13] 'Presupposition, Supervaluation and Free Logic'.

[14] 'Supervaluations: Identity, Existence, and Individual Concepts'.

which provokes these questions is due not so much to indecision on Quine's part about what the correct evaluation policy is for statements containing assumed irreferential singular terms as it is to his indifference. From the logical point of view any policy is as good as any other so long as consistency with the laws of logic is preserved, and also with the 'fact' that statements of the form '*s* exists', where '*s*' is replaceable by an irreferential singular term, are false; from the logical point of view all such sentences, with the exception just noted, are treated as 'don't cares'. Indeed, free logicians have canvassed the various possibilities over the last two decades, though they do not regard such statements as 'don't cares'. One reason for this is their disagreement with Quine about what the logical point of view is. Another reason is having goals different from Quine's, for instance, providing a semantical foundation for scientific fictional discourse ('Vulcan', 'John's ego'), or for nonscientific fictional discourse ('Sherlock Holmes', 'the winged horse ridden by Bellerophon'). Two examples will suffice.

First, in the Scales–Burge approach, if a statement is simple and contains at least one irreferential singular term, it is false. An example is (4) 'Vulcan rotates'. If it is a complex statement, then the truth-value of the statement depends on whether the irreferential singular terms have 'primary' or 'secondary' occurrence in them, approximately in Russell's sense of the words. For example, in 'Heimdal is a nonexistent', 'Heimdal' has primary occurrence and the statement is false, but in 'It is not the case that Heimdal is an existent', 'Heimdal' has secondary occurrence and the statement is true. In other complex statements containing irreferential singular terms, the truth-value could be false even though the singular term has secondary occurrence – just as for Russell.

A second example of an approach recognizing irreferential singular terms but with complete evaluation rules is that presented by van Fraassen and me in our book, *Derivation and Counterexample*.[15] There, we advance the notion of a 'story' and say, in effect, that the truth-value of a simple or complex non-

[15] Dickensen, Encino, Ca., 1971.

existential statement containing irreferential singular terms depends upon whether or not it is contained in the story. The statement

> Sherlock Holmes is a detective

is true because that sentence is contained in the 'story' and the same holds for

> Sherlock Holmes is a detective or he is an imposter.

Quine's indifference and free logicians' passion notwithstanding, the fact that there are several possible ways of evaluating statements containing irreferential singular terms does not undercut either the legitimacy or the importance of the questions initiating this discussion of the truth-values to be ascribed to simple statements containing irreferential singular terms. The fact that there are many ways of evaluating such statements of predication suggests that there is no unique association between evaluation rules and predication. This suggestion is bolstered by the earlier observation that there is a sense of predication common to many free logicians, for example, of the Scales–Burge or the Lambert–van Fraassen kind, even though the former evaluate (6) as false, and the latter evaluate it both differently and as true.

To return to the two questions posed above: first, is predication merely a syntactical matter for the $\overline{CT}$ theorist? No. That predication is not simply the result of joining singular term(s) and general term to form a statement, even in the special case of irreferential singular terms, is inherent in this fact; some who espouse $\overline{CT}$ would surely deny that

> (8) The commissioner is looking for Tom Jones

is a predication, and others might very well deny that

> (9) Heimdal exists

is a predication, and, indeed, some might deny that both are predications. But (8) and (9) are statements joining general terms to singular terms, some of which, let us assume, are irreferential. So it is not the case that every subscriber to $\overline{\text{CT}}$ regards every statement resulting from the joining of irreferential singular term(s) and general term to have the form of a predication – even vacuously by virtue of a singular term failing to refer.

Quine, for example, thinks no statements of the form

(10) The commissioner is looking for...,

opaquely interpreted, are predicational,[16] no matter what kind of singular term fills the blank space. The reason is that even if the singular term replacing the blank space in (10) were to refer, the statement would *not* be either true (or false) of the specified object, and thus the truth-value of statements of the form in (10), whatever they may be, could not be so dependent, a condition required for a statement to be a predication. The same goes for statements such as (9) – at least under easily imaginable circumstances. Suppose, for instance, a certain philosopher were to accept (*a*) a sharp distinction between (grammatically) proper names and definite descriptions, and also to accept (*b*) Russell's view in *Principia Mathematica* that one can assert existence of an individual described but not of the individual named though they be one and the same individual.[17] This philosopher, it seems, treats existence contexts as nonextensional in the sense of Quine.[18] So, if the singular term in the place of the blank space in '... exists' *were* to refer (in a sense of 'refer' appropriate both to names and descriptions), then 'exists' *would not* be either true (or false) of the object referred to. So statements of the form '... exists' – (7), for instance – would not be predications.

This discussion also provides the answer to the second question about the nonsyntactical means appealed to by those

[16] *Word and Object*, pp. 142–3.
[17] Whitehead and Russell, *Principia Mathematica*, 2nd edn, p. 174.
[18] Church has recently urged that singular existence contexts be treated as cases of 'ungerade usage'. Whether this recommendation amounts to 'nonextensional' in the sense of Quine is not discussed, but I doubt it. See A. Church, 'Outline of a Revised Formulation of the Logic of Sense and Denotation' (part II), *Noûs*, 8 (1974), p. 143.

C$\overline{\text{T}}$ theorists who regard some statements containing irreferential singular terms as nonpredications: the reason why (2),

> The spheroid which is such that it is not a spheroid is spherical,

is a predication is that *were* 'The spheroid which is such that it is not a spheroid' to refer *successfully*, then the truth-value of (2) *would* depend on whether the general term 'spherical' is true (or false) of the thing so specified. And similarly for (6).

The entire discussion can be generalized. Suppose, in fact, a certain C$\overline{\text{T}}$ theorist to regard *every* statement constructed of general term and irreferential singular term(s) to be a predication (*contra*, for instance, Quine). Then the very idea of an expression being a singular term, an expression that *purports* to refer, suggests a logical role not properly explained by considering merely the category of logical grammar to which it belongs. The reason our C$\overline{\text{T}}$ theorist thinks (2) is a predication is because he believes that the expression 'The spheroid which is such that it is not a spheroid' plays the same logical role in (2) as is played by the demonstrative 'That' in

(1) That is spherical,

which is a predication in virtually everyone's theory. That role is to specify an object for the rest of the statement to talk about. But, for the C$\overline{\text{T}}$ theorist, playing that logical role does not entail performing it successfully, a demand indeed required by the CT theorist. So, if one replaces 'That' in (1) by the singular term 'The spheroid which is such that it is not a spheroid', even though assumed to be irreferential, one does not thereby get a statement, (2), with a different logical form.

The semantic import of the phrase 'playing the same logical role' so far as predication is concerned is more properly expressed in the subjunctive mood. The C$\overline{\text{T}}$ core principle of predication can be put in this way: predication joins an n-place general term to n singular terms to form a statement which would be true or false according as the n-place general term is true (or false) of the n-tuple of objects referred to by the n

singular terms were they to refer. There is indeed a sense in which predication even for the C$\overline{\text{T}}$ theorist is associated with an evaluation rule. But whereas the CT theorist presumes certain conditions of reference to obtain, the C$\overline{\text{T}}$ theorist does not. For him the purposes of logic are fulfilled when one expresses how a statement would be evaluated were certain conditions to obtain; that is what the logical form of the statement is.

Two fairly straightforward remarks about C$\overline{\text{T}}$, then, are these. First, knowing that a statement has the logical form of a predication does not entail knowledge of the truth-value of that statement. This, of course, is true in the case of CT also. But the point here is that when a predicational statement contains an irreferential singular term, the particular *way* in which that statement is assessed for truth-value may vary considerably from one C$\overline{\text{T}}$ theorist to another, partly depending upon the purpose at hand, be it an analysis of fictional discourse or an analysis of attribution, or whatever it may be. One of the values of the C$\overline{\text{T}}$ core principle of predication, it can be urged, lies in the clear perspective it brings to the question of what the purposes behind the ways of evaluating statements for truth-value are.

Second, it is clear that the C$\overline{\text{T}}$ core principle of predication is weaker than the CT core principle of predication: any statement which is a predication on the latter conception is a predication on the former, but not necessarily the other way round. Virtually identical classes of predications, of course, can be secured by artificial means such as the Frege–Carnap method of assigning denotata to irreferential singular terms. Without the latter kind of strategem, (2) would not be a predication by CT but would be so by C$\overline{\text{T}}$, on the tediously cited assumption that 'The spheroid which is such that it is not a spheroid' is an irreferential singular term.

To summarize, the key facts of this section are, first, that the statement (2),

The spheroid which is such that it is not a spheroid is

spherical,

where 'the spheroid which is such that it is not a spheroid' is counted irreferential, is regarded by some as a predication, and, second, that in this group there are those that may nevertheless disagree about the truth-value of (2). The key motivation for treating the statement as a predication is that the singular term occupying the grammatical subject position in (2) plays the same logical role as 'that' in (1),

That is spherical,

and that role is to refer to the object which the rest of the sentence is about. The crucial caveat is that playing that role does not imply that reference is always successful, any more than playing the role of president implies that it is done successfully. The key implication is that there is no unique relation between the conception of predication issuing from these facts, motives and caveats, and truth-value assessment. On the other hand, this does not mean that, for a given exponent of the nontraditional core principle $C\overline{T}$, there cannot be a uniform way of assessing the truth-value of all predications. It does suggest, however, that there are nonlogical factors involved in truth-value assessment. Finally, the concept of predication reflected in $C\overline{T}$ does not imply that predication is purely a syntactical matter.

III. THE NONEXTENSIONALITY OF $C\overline{T}$

$C\overline{T}$ is nonextensional in at least one fairly common and nontrivial sense of the word. The sense concerned holds that a theory is nonextensional if there are coextensive general terms of the theory such that substitution of one for the other in some statements of the theory changes the truth-value of those statements.[19] Construing 'object' in its broadest sense, where the

---

[19] If the extensions of singular terms are identified with their referents (at least in direct discourse), then $C\overline{T}$ is trivially nonextensional in the sense that not all singular terms have extensions. If by 'nonextensionality' one means that Fregean maxim that the extension of a complex expression is not a function of the extensions

extension of a general term is the set of objects of which a general term is true, a well-worn example of a nonextensional theory is the theory of possibility and necessity. Thus, the general terms 'is the number of the planets' and 'is nine' are true of the same objects, and hence have the same extension. But though the statement 'Necessarily everything which is nine is nine' is true, the statement resulting from substitution of 'is the number of the planets' for 'is nine' in its first occurrence yields the false statement 'Necessarily everything which is the number of the planets is nine.'

So consider in general a theory with the core principle C$\overline{\text{T}}$ obeying these conditions. First, it must contain at least one irreferential singular term, for example, 'The spheroid which is such that it is not a spheroid'. Second, there is a general term true of exactly the universe of objects, whatever its constituency; the general term might simply be 'object' or perhaps 'is some object'. The expression 'The spheroid which is such that it is not a spheroid', not referring at all, certainly cannot specify any object. Consider now the statements 'The spheroid which is such that it is not a spheroid is an object' or 'The spheroid which is such that it is not a spheroid is some object.' Certainly neither of these can be true on any reasonable assumptions about reference and truth. But, nevertheless, they qualify as predications because were 'The spheroid which is such that it is not a spheroid' to refer, then the truth-value of the statements in question would surely depend on whether

of its parts, it depends upon what 'function' in this principle means and otherwise how broadly the expression is construed, whether C$\overline{\text{T}}$ is nonextensional. See K. Lambert, 'Being and Being So'. Moreover, the senses of 'extension' alluded to above and in the body of the text concern languages or theories or linguistic entities, and not nonlinguistic things. But many believe the term also properly distinguishes among things, say, for example, sets (extensional) and properties (nonextensional). And it is not at all obvious whether an extensional theory as defined in the text necessitates an ontology comprising only extensional entities. Frege's theories suggest otherwise. For senses are allegedly nonextensional entities, but Frege apparently requires universal substitution principles for all kinds of expressions in all kinds of contexts. That is, he does not permit violation of the *salva veritate* condition on substitutions of any kinds of term or expression. Finally, the characterization of nonextensionality in the body of the text is essentially Quine's; *Word and Object*, p. 151.

the general terms 'object' and 'is some object' were true (or false) of the referent so specified – trivially true, of course, in each case in virtue of the understanding about what the general terms in question are true of, that is, the members of the universe of discourse itself. Notice now that under these assumptions the complex general terms 'spherical object' and 'spherical if an object' are coextensive because they are true (or false) of exactly the same objects, namely everything that is spherical (or nothing that is spherical). What is to be established is that no matter what truth-value the statement 'The spheroid which is such that it is not a spheroid is spherical' has, if any, substitution of coextensive predicates for the predicate 'spherical' in the statement 'The spheroid which is such that it is not a spheroid is spherical' does not always preserve truth-value.

There are three cases to consider depending on what truth-value the statement

> The spheroid which is such that it is not a spheroid is spherical

has: true, false, or no truth-value at all.

First, consider the case where the statement in question is true. Then substitution of the general term 'spherical object' for 'spherical' yields the false statement 'The spheroid which is such that it is not a spheroid is a spherical object', given the falsity of 'The spheroid which is such that it is not a spheroid is an object'. Second, let the statement in question be false. Then substitution of the general term 'spherical if an object' for the general term 'spherical' yields the true statement 'The spheroid which is such that it is not a spheroid is spherical if an object'. Finally, suppose the centerpiece statement to be truth-valueless. Then substitution, for example, of the general term 'spherical object' for the general term 'spherical' yields the false statement 'The spheroid which is such that it is not a spheroid is a spherical object' under any reasonable interpretation of the suppressed conjunction 'and' in the complex predicate 'spherical object'.

The argument can be given substance – no pun intended – if one imagines a C$\overline{\text{T}}$ theorist – Quine, for example – who recognizes only beings as objects. Then the general term 'object' is replaced by 'being' on the ground that 'being' is true of entity b just in case b is a being. (Compare 'true' in 'true of the proposition that Meinong is Austrian just in case the proposition that Meinong is Austrian is true'.) Quine holds that 'The spheroid which is such that it is not a spheroid is a being (exists)' is false, and it surely is the case that the statement in question is a predication given C$\overline{\text{T}}$. It should be emphasized again that nothing depends on taking the particular general term 'being' ('exists') to be true of (the lowest level of) objects; for the argument will go through by switching to clearly acceptable general terms such as 'is the same as some being'.

Ever since Frege, and especially in the recent writings of Quine, the property of extensionality has assumed major importance in contemporary analytic philosophy. In fact, it has assumed the character almost of a criterion of adequacy for philosophical theories in some quarters. Part of the reason for this concerns a presumed connection between objectivity and extensionality, the belief that if a theory is nonextensional, or cannot be 'reformulated' in extensional terms, as the nonextensional idiom of quotation can be replaced by the extensional idiom of spelling,[20] then the objectivity of the theory is suspect. I pass no firm judgment on this belief here. Yet it seems clear that the traditional theory of predication is extensional, and thus one might choose this approach over the nontraditional approach on grounds other than the direct association it allows between logical form and evaluation rules afforded by the theory of predication based on CT. But there is a definite sacrifice in doing so. For the theory of predication based on CT fosters an illusion, the illusion that the reasons for adopting a particular set of truth conditions are logical in the sense of *formal* logic, and thus that differences in evaluation rules reflect differences in beliefs about what is valid on formal

---

[20] Cf. W. V. Quine, 'The Scope and Language of Science', in *The Ways of Paradox*, Random House, New York, 1966.

grounds alone. Contemporary philosophers ought at least to be sensitive to the fact that reasons for adopting particular evaluation rules often depend on other than logical goals and in fact may conflict with the former sometimes. Such is the result, for example, of the practical decision to set the conditional 'if A then B' true, when 'A' is false and 'B' is true, at least according to some of the pioneers in the analysis of relevant implication. For they hold that the validity of an inference of the form

A;
So, if B then B,

a consequence in part of the practical policy above, is not consonant with the belief that what is valid in formal logic should be valid by form alone.[21]

Again, I pass no judgment here on the claims of the believers in relevant implication; the point is only that the belief that formal validity underdetermines evaluation rules (truth conditions) is not a new doctrine in philosophical logic, that a theory of predication based on $C\overline{T}$ suggests only a new vestige of an old belief.

IV. INDEPENDENCE AND $C\overline{T}$

Returning to the principle of independence the question arises about its relation to $C\overline{T}$. As suggested early in the last chapter, there is no essential connection between the two principles: some $C\overline{T}$ theorists implicitly or explicitly reject the principle of independence, others accept it. Ronald Scales and Tyler Burge, for example, explicitly reject the principle, and Quine implicitly rejects it.[22]

Recall first that the principle of independence, the principle that the argument from

---

[21] A. R. Anderson and Nuel D. Belnap, Jr., 'Tautological Entailments', *Philosophical Studies*, 13 (1962), pp. 9–24.

[22] Ronald Scales, *Attribution and Reference*, University of Michigan Microfilms, 1968; Burge, 'Singular Terms and Truth'; Quine, *Word and Object*.

$(EP)P$ is possessed by s

to

s has being

is invalid, is incompatible with the validity of argument from

Gs

to

s has being.

(Here 'G' takes as substituends the general term correlate of the singular term which is a substituend of the variable 'P' – 'spherical' for 'sphericity', for instance.) This was proved in the last chapter. So acceptance of the validity of

Gs;
So, s has being

implies rejection of the invalidity

$(EP)P$ is possessed by s;
So, s has being,

hence of the principle of independence. The argument

Gs;
So, s has being

is what is directly at issue (or more accurately the argument from

$G^n s_1 \ldots s_n$

to

So, s_1 has being & $\ldots$ & s_n has being,

where 'G^n' takes as substitution n-place general terms and '$s_1 \ldots s_n$' are replaced by n singular terms. Discussion will be carried on by means of the simpler schema). 'Gs' is, by agreement, the form of a simple predication, and what Scales and

Burge explicitly accept is the validity of

> *Gs*;
> So, *s* has being,

or its more complex brethren.

Scales views the validity of the inference pattern above as a reflection in more current talk of the old metaphysical doctrine that nothing (= nothing which has no being) can have no properties. Burge adduces reasons based on the theory of truth (in the Tarski style) in support of his acceptance of the validity of the inference pattern in question. In Meinongian language this might be called the principle of the *interdependence of being so and being* – or simply the principle of interdependence. The ontological attitude in both cases is uncompromisingly Russellian; the objects are precisely the subsistents (existents).

Quine's attitude, however, at least in *Methods of Logic*, is not so metaphysically oriented. He thinks that the simplest policy for treating 'don't cares', predications containing at least one singular term referring to no existent, is to assign them the truth-value false; other purposes, he acknowledges, might dictate other truth-value policies (as in his *Set Theory and Its Logic*) and hence a different attitude toward the principle of interdependence. But, of course, he everywhere subscribes explicitly to the ontological policy that there are no objects but the actual ones.

On the other hand, there are $C\overline{T}$ theorists who accept the principle of independence, and hence reject the validity of

> *Gs*;
> So, *s* has being.

Bas van Fraassen is one such person; another is Ermanno Bencivenga, and I, too, have long espoused such a view.[23]

All of the representatives of $C\overline{T}$ so far mentioned are free logicians. (Free logic comes in for an extensive discussion in

---

[23] Bas van Fraassen's (and my) view is expressed in one form in our book *Derivation and Counterexample*; Ermanno Bencivenga's view is in his 'Free Semantics' (forthcoming).

the next chapter.) But the association is not unique. There are
C$\overline{T}$ theorists who do not espouse free logic but who accept the
principle of independence. Terence Parsons (in his *Nonexistent
Objects*) is a case in point.

The nuances of these various positions can be made clearer
by an example. Consider, again,

(6) The spheroid which is such that it is not a spheroid is
the spheroid which is such that it is not a spheroid.

Given the Scales–Burge position, the falsehood of (6) *follows*
from the principle of interdependence. But the truth of (6) does
not follow from acceptance of the principle of independence.
That

> Gs;
> So, s has being

is accepted as invalid is no evidence that (6) is true. One
might, for example, given the nonsubsistence of the spheroid
which is such that it is not a spheroid, judge (6) truth-valueless
or even false. Parsons, for example, adopts the latter policy
even though he is a C$\overline{T}$ theorist who supports the principle of
independence. How? Because he regards as valid the inference
pattern

> Gs;
> So, s is an object,

but rejects the objecthood of the spheroid which is such that it
is not a spheroid. Thus, it is clear that C$\overline{T}$ theorists who
believe in the truth of (6) must have independent grounds for
believing this even though the truth of (6) is often used by
some to support adoption of the principle of independence.
The very most that follows from the principle of independence
is that some predications are true, but which ones is a matter
that requires appeal to other considerations.

The upshot of these latest observations on the principle of
independence is that it has no inextricable connection with the
theory of predication based on the core principle C$\overline{T}$. Just as in

the case of the core principle CT, where one's being regarded as a traditionalist is indeed greatly affected by adoption or rejection of the principle of independence – Meinong and Russell, respectively – so a $\overline{\text{CT}}$ theorist can be a 'traditionalist', in another sense of the word, by rejecting the principle of independence. As these last two chapters have sought to show, one's position on predication can, and often does, have more to do with the constraints than with essence.

A summary of the discussion in this chapter is very much in order. The key point is that the evaluation rule (or rules) associated with predication is (or are) a mixture of logical and nonlogical factors. Consider, for example, the evaluation rule appropriate to the Scales–Burge view. A predication

   Gs

is true just in case s has being and G is true of s; it is false just in case either s does not have being or s has being and G is false of s. Whether s has being or not is often a factual matter. Thus, if 'G' is replaced by 'rotates' and 's' by 'Vulcan', the resulting predication is false in virtue of the *fact* that Vulcan has no being. But the predicational status of

   (4) Vulcan rotates

does not in the least depend upon this fact. The assertion that the statement in question has the logical form of a predication has the following force, so far as evaluation is concerned. If certain conditions were to obtain (that 'Vulcan' refers, for instance), then the truth-value of (4) would be ascertained by seeing whether the general term 'rotates' is true (or false) of the specified object. In other words, logical form does influence evaluation in the context of certain specified conditions, but it is powerless to guarantee these conditions. How to evaluate predications, therefore, in the face of unsatisfied reference conditions can be (and is) dependent on many different and often conflicting interests, many of which one would be hard put to classify as logical.

The absence of the demand that the singular terms of a

statement refer in a theory of predication having C̄T̄ as its core is the key to the solution of the problem that opened this chapter. The intuition that (2),

> The spheroid which is such that it is not a spheroid is spherical,

is a predication because it has the same logical form as (1),

> That is spherical,

which is indisputably predicational, does not conflict with a theory of predication based on C̄T̄ outlined in the preceding pages simply because there is no demand in such a theory that a predication always contain only referential singular terms. According to C̄T̄-founded theory, (1) is predicational, and that conception does not require that 'The spheroid which is such that it is not a spheroid' actually refer.

Any theory of predication having C̄T̄ as its core is, as was proved one section back, nonextensional in one widely understood sense of the word. Further, because of its reticence on the truth-value, and its manner of assessment, in cases where the reference conditions are not met, it threatens the conception of logical form as identifiable with manner of evaluation. These features may make one feel uneasy about C̄T̄-founded theories, but that feeling must be offset by the illumination such theories shed on the factors involved in truth-value assessment. And it is also offset by the difficulty of constructing an alternative theory of predication without C̄T̄ using resources (a) acceptable to Meinongians and (b) adequate to the solution of the problem that opened this chapter produced by the irreferential singular term 'The spheroid which is such that it is not a spheroid'. Seen in this light, C̄T̄-generated theories of predication are provocative and promising.

INDEPENDENCE AND FREE LOGIC

I. FREE LOGIC: PRELIMINARY CONSIDERATIONS

In the previous two chapters the connection between the principle of independence and the theory of predication was examined. The argument was made that the influence of that principle on the theory of predication, though important, is not seminal; neither its acceptance nor its rejection is entailed by the core of the traditional theory – nor, for that matter, by the core of the nontraditional theory discussed in Chapter 4. It is, of course, the key respect in which Meinong's theory of predication is nontraditional, but that fact should not cloud the equally important respect in which Meinong's views are every bit as traditional as those of his near contemporaries, Frege and Russell.

In this chapter, we turn to a subject matter of some importance in the current analytic environment, and on which the principle of independence does exert an essential influence in precisely the sense enunciated above; acceptance of the principle is entailed by certain accounts of that subject matter, and not entailed by others. The subject matter, broadly speaking, is philosophical logic; in particular, it is that branch of philosophical logic called the logic of singular terms, and the accounts in question are the various accounts qualifying as *free logics*. I want to begin by setting the discussion of free logic(s) in a more or less familiar background, and will then discuss in more detail the character of those theories of terms falling within this two-and-a-half-decade-old approach. The connection of the principle of independence with free logic will emerge in due course.

What is novel about free logic is its position on singular terms and hence on inferences turning on statements including such terms. It breaks sharply with the traditional approaches to singular inference in modern logic, the Fregeian approach on the one hand, and the Russellian approach on the other. All these theories, by the way, are about expressions in actual or reformed natural languages such as English, German, French and so on, or at least in an actual or reformed fragment of natural language.

What distinguishes these various traditions? Let us look at some examples. Consider the four expressions

(1) Leo Sachse,
(2) The president of the United States in 1979,
(3) My mother's favorite joke,
(4) Pegasus

and the schema

(5) There exists something the same as s, where s takes as substituends singular terms.[1]

Frege's position was, in effect, that (a) the expressions (1)–(4), all of them members of the class of expressions he called *Namen*, are what we now call singular terms, (b) each of the expressions (1)–(4) can be legitimately substituted into the variable 's' in the validating schema (5), and (c) the resulting instances, for example the statement

(6) There exists something the same as Pegasus,

are true. Frege, in contrast to Meinong, but in agreement with many free logicians, considered the term 'Pegasus' to be really irreferential, but thought it both dangerous[2] and odious to

---

[1] Throughout this chapter it is well to remember that 'exists' is synonymous with 'subsists'. The former expression is the conventional one used in discussion of free logic. It is odd to speak of logics free of 'subsistence assumptions', even though it is synonymous with 'existence assumptions'. This chapter, in a sense, is played by ear.

[2] Concerning the danger of bearerless singular terms, Frege said, 'It is customary in logic texts to warn against the ambiguity of expressions as a source of fallacies. I

permit bearerless singular terms in a language designed for the formulation and analysis of problems in science and philosophy. So he arbitrarily assigned to singular terms like 'Pegasus' a referent, a certain set in one version of the theory, but a chosen individual in another version of the theory. This course has the result that since the statement in (6) turns out to be true, the statement 'Pegasus exists', which is not true, cannot be paraphrased by it.

Russell's view was that (a) *none* of the expressions (1)–(4) are singular terms, (b) none are legitimate substitution instances of '*s*' in the validating schema (5), and (c), *contra* Frege, the statement (6) is in fact false. Accordingly, in Russell's view, the false statement 'Pegasus exists', containing the grammatically proper (but logically improper) name 'Pegasus', is acceptable shorthand for (6).

The free logician believes that (a) each of the expressions (1)–(4) is a singular term, (b) each expression is a legitimate substitution of the schema in (5), but (c) the statement in (6) is false. Hence, as in the case of Russell, the statement 'Pegasus exists' is properly paraphraseable by statement (6). In contrast to Frege, however, whose position on the logical form of the statement in (6) the free logician shares, the free logician does not arbitrarily assign any existent object to expressions such as 'Pegasus'.

These different attitudes about how to treat expressions such as (1)–(4) can be summed up in this way. In the interest of maintaining the validating character of the schema in (5), Frege and Russell brush· aside one or another of the

deem it at least as appropriate to issue a warning against proper names that have no nominata. The history of mathematics has many a tale to tell of errors which originated from this source. The demagogic misuse is as close (perhaps closer) at hand as in the case of ambiguous expressions. 'The will of the people' may serve as an example in this regard; for it is easily established that there is no generally accepted nominatum of that expression. Thus it is obviously not without importance to obstruct once for all the source of these errors, at least as regards their occurrence in science'. (See G. Frege, 'On Sense and Nominatums', in H. Feigl and W. Sellars (eds.), *Readings in Philosophical Analysis* (Appleton-Century-Crofts, New York, 1949), p. 96.) This passage shows, by the way, that Frege's method of the artificial reference is not motivated simply by mathematical concerns, as is so often alleged.

appearances exhibited by the statement in (6); Frege brushes aside the appearance of falsehood, and Russell brushes aside the appearance that the statement in (6) has the logical form of the statement in (5). Free logicians, on the other hand, in the interests of saving appearances, reject the conviction that the schema in (5) is validating.

Meinong's views on the termhood of (1)–(4), and the logical form and truth-value of the statement (6), duplicate the views of the free logician. Is Meinong, then, one of the original if unannounced free logicians? No; and the reasons why he is not are philosophically interesting.

Free logicians fall into two distinct groups according to the attitude they adopt towards the irreferential status of expressions such as 'Pegasus' (or 'Vulcan', the name of the purported but nonexistent planet). One group holds them to be irreferential; the other group, like Meinong, holds them to refer to no existent entity but nevertheless to be referential. This latter position has been thought to be essentially Meinongian, and so it has been believed that some free logicians were Meinongian. But the belief is oversimplified. The true Meinongian, as previous pages make clear, quantifies over nonexistent objects; he acknowledges both the sense and the truth of statements such as 'No round square exists', 'There are beingless objects that are spherical and there are beingless objects that are not spherical', and so on. No free logician, however, quantifies over beingless objects. The distinction is important because there is a large body of analytic philosophers who believe an entity cannot aspire to full objecthood unless counted – in Quine's words – among the values of the bound variables. If you say Pegasus is an object, then you cannot deny him the right to be counted among the entities supporting the truth of the statement 'There are beingless objects', for instance.

In his essay 'Advice on Modal Logic', Dana Scott acknowledges the association between quantification and objecthood, but nevertheless recognizes a realm of object-like entities whose purpose is to help regularize our language, and over which no quantifier ranges.[3] These entities are *virtual objects*; they are rather like second-class citizens, who are clearly recognizable as such but who do not enjoy the rights of complete personhood. So free logicians who recognize an 'outer domain' of beingless entities as referents for 'Pegasus' and 'Vulcan' are treating these entities as virtual objects rather than as fully endowed *beingless* objects. To sum up, Meinong is no free logician because he believes 'Pegasus' and 'Vulcan' refer to objects in the full sense of the word, where 'fullness of sense' is determined by the willingness to make *general* claims about them, to quantify over them. No free logician goes *that* far. Nevertheless some free logicians subscribe to some of his beliefs – in particular, the principle of independence – as will be clear shortly.

The motivations for free logic are diverse, and they come in layers. The deepest ones, sporadic, half-conscious and vague, seldom justify beliefs. These motives – let us call them the primordial ones – even if not always good reasons for one's beliefs, nevertheless often mitigate them. For example, there is a primordial intuition that logic is a tool of the philosopher and ideally should be neutral with respect to philosophical truth, just as the various mathematical tools available to the empirical scientist – calculus, statistics, algebra, or what have you – are presumed neither to create nor to predetermine what the empirical facts are. Logic, like the tools of scientists, is used to help decide among the various opinions which is the truth – or at least it should according to this intuition. So if there are preconditions to logic that have the effect of settling what exists and what does not exist, they ought to be eliminated

---

[3] 'The possibility of introducing virtual entities is unlimited and for the most part relatively unexplored. They are not to be regarded as ghosts but rather as *ideal objects* introduced to enhance the regularity of our language. By using the names of these entities we often find a simple formulation that avoids a confusing proliferation of cases. In the ordinary theory of real numbers $\pm \infty$ are excellent examples of useful ideal points; in projective geometry, the points at infinity; in set theory, the virtual classes ... The next question is: should we quantify over virtual objects? I think the answer should be a firm no. ... If we have come to value the virtual entities so highly that we want to quantify over them, then we have passed to a *new* theory with a *new* ontology (and with new virtuals also!)' ('Advice on Modal Logic', in Karel Lambert (ed.), *Philosophical Problems in Logic*).

because they corrupt the ideal of logic as a philosophical tool. Many admit the grip of this primordial intuition on that mildly sentimental phosphorescence that guides each of us. But it would be a mistake to think all free logicians fall into this group. So to understand the whys and wherefores of free logic it is better to look at particular motivations for free logic operating nearer the surface of conscious deliberation than to concentrate on the more primitive inhabitants of the philosophical ooze.

Motivations for free logic with more appearance of justification are plentiful. There is, of course, dissatisfaction with the traditional approaches to singular inference, but as a matter of historical fact this item has more often been a consequence of, rather than a reason for, adopting a free logic. Historically, free logic arose from other sources for other reasons in a mood of Cartesian independence. One such source is the asymmetry in the treatment of general terms and singular terms in modern symbolic logic.

Consider, for example, the inference pattern

Every F is G;
So, there exists an F which is G.

'Traditional' logic recognized the validity of any inference of this pattern. It staved off the charge of inconsistency in the face of instances such as

Every body on which there are no external forces acting moves uniformly in a straight line;
So, there exists a body on which there are no external forces acting which moves in a straight line,

an argument with a true premise and a false conclusion, by restricting 'F' and 'G' to general terms true of at least one existing thing. Modern logic, however, for well-known reasons, rejects the validating character of the above inference pattern and tolerates general terms such as 'body on which there is no external force acting' and 'spheroid which is such that it is not a spheroid', general terms true of no existing object. Curiously, however, the attitude of modern logic toward the inference pattern

Every existing thing is F;
So, s is F

is like that of the 'traditional' logic toward the inference pattern earlier described. Modern logic treats this new pattern as validating even in the face of counterinstances such as

Every existing thing exists;
So, Pegasus exists.

Some logicians believe that the reasons behind the modern rejection of the earlier inference pattern are just as compelling in the case of the latter inference pattern. So they reject it, and tolerate singular terms referring to no existing object such as the singular terms 'Pegasus' and 'Vulcan'.

So here is one source of free logic. The idea is that the methods of logic ought to apply to reasoning containing expressions that one *may not be sure* refer to any existing objects – as in the case of those astronomers who used the name 'Vulcan' in their explanations and conjectures before the purported object was determined not to exist. And they even ought to apply to reasoning containing expressions that one *knows in fact do not refer* to any existing object – such as the reasoning of physicists using the definite description 'the body at position P on which no external forces are acting'.

Another motivation for free logic lies in a widespread view about logical truth. Consider the standard of logical truth first promulgated by Bolzano, but resurrected and more limpidly stated by Quine. The idea is this. Assume the catalogue of the words and phrases of a language to be divided into two classes: (a) the logical words and phrases ('and', 'it is not the case that', for instance) and (b) the nonlogical (or descriptive) words or phrases ('Carter', 'man', for instance). Then the logical truths of that language are those true statements that can be turned into falsehoods only by replacements of its logical words (or phrases) by other words (or phrases). In other words, if, roughly speaking, you uniformly replace descriptive words (or phrases) of the appropriate kind by descriptive words (or phrases) of that kind you cannot turn the statement from a truth to a falsehood. For example, the statement

There exists something that is a horse or is not a horse

is logically true, but the statement

There exists something that is a horse

is not, because the second but not the first becomes false when the descriptive wordtype 'horse' is replaced everywhere by the descriptive wordtype 'unicorn'.

The Bolzano–Quine standard of logical truth is often thought to be a way of capturing the intuition that the truths of logic are truths solely by virtue of their form. Now it turns out that despite the potential counterexample in the statement (6), the statement

(7) There exists something the same as Carter

is conventionally treated as logically true even by those who espouse the Bolzano-Quine criterion of logical truth.

Quine, in contrast to Russell, holds that expressions such as 'Pegasus' are genuine singular terms[4] but treats them as inconveniences. He believes their introduction into what he calls the 'canonical language' results in various inelegancies and so, in the interests of theoretical smoothness and simplicity, ought to be disallowed.

The canonical language purports to be an idiom sufficient to the legitimate needs of science. The smoothness of that idiom would be affected, for example, by the admission of statements such as

(8) Heimdal sings

---

[4] *Word and Object*, p. 177.

which, being neither true nor false (Quine believes), introduce truth-value gaps into the canonical language. But adoption of another truth-value besides truth and falsity to fill the gaps would complicate the two-valued canonical idiom. The truth-value gaps are caused by irreferential singular terms such as 'Pegasus', and, Quine notes, would not arise if two-valued canonical paraphrases for natural language statements containing them were available. Here Russell is ready with an answer. His technique of definite description now provides the needed paraphrases, and indeed they are paraphrases in which singular terms such as 'Pegasus' do not survive.

A major complaint against Quine's approach is that it sacrifices the truth for convenience; if the expression 'Pegasus' is counted as a genuine but irreferential singular term, as Quine counts it, then, by the Bolzano–Quine standard of logical truth, *it is true* that the statement (7),

There exists something the same as Carter,

is not logically true. So one would expect this fact about logic, a subject which, for Quine, is an important ingredient in the conceptual scheme of science, to be reflected in the canonical language. But since singular terms have, for reasons of convenience, been banished from the canonical language, neither the nonlogical truth of statement (7) nor the reason for judging it not logically true can be represented in the canonical idiom. This dialectic raises the question whether the canonical idiom presented by Quine really does succeed in one of its major goals, that of clarifying the conceptual scheme of science. Here, then, is a second motivation for free logic, namely, the devising of a canonical idiom more reflective of the actual scheme of science, and more adequate to the needs of science and philosophy.

A third source of motivation for free logic concerns the foundations of modal and temporal discourse. Consider the most popular foundation for these sorts of discourse – the possible worlds account – the inspiration for which is Leibniz in general conception if not in specific detail.[5] This kind of foundation provides a straightforward account of metaphysically necessary truth as truth in (or of) *all* possible worlds, and metaphysically possible truth as truth in (or of) some possible worlds. If the possible worlds are thought of as temporal stages, then temporally necessary truth amounts to truth in all temporally possible stages. Now, if one supposes, as seems natural, that the objects existing in one possible world may not exist in another world, then it seems proper to explicate the statement 'Carter really exists' by the statement 'Carter exists in the real world', and to explicate the statement 'Pegasus might have existed but does not really' by the statement 'Pegasus exists in some possible world but not in the real world'. This style of explication has implications for statements about the reference of singular terms. For example, it implies that the singular term 'Carter' refers to an existent in the real world, but the singular term 'Pegasus' does not.

The upshot of these views about the reference of the singular terms: 'Carter' and 'Pegasus' is, of course, that the statement (6),

There exists something the same as Pegasus,

is false of the real world, and hence that the conditional

(9) If it is not the case that there exists something the same as Pegasus, then there exists something that doesn't exist

is false of the real world. The conditional is thus a counterexample to the classical principle of *particularization*, a principle rejected in free logic. And the opinion here is reinforced by

[5] 'What I mean by the phrase "in general conception if not in specific detail" is this: It is conceivable that one might explicate necessary truth as truth in all possible worlds – in the general spirit of Leibniz's account of necessity, but adopt a view of possible worlds differing from Leibniz's (or a Leibniz-like) view. For example, Leibniz apparently holds that it is not true that a given possible object can occur in more than one metaphysically possible world let alone in all of them. This conviction is incompatible with the conception of the set of possible worlds as consisting of the same objects in each but differing only with respect to their configuration – a kind of popcorn machine picture of metaphysical atomism' (R. Thomason, 'Modal Logic and Metaphysics', in Karel Lambert (ed.), *The Logical Way of Doing Things*, p. 127).

consideration of names like 'Pegasus' and definite descriptions such as 'the spheroid which is such that it is not a spheroid', which taken as singular terms, refer to no existent in *any* possible world. The moral is that the quantificational part of the correct modal or temporal logic is free logic.

The historically important sources of motivations discussed above certainly do not exhaust the possible or actual sources of motivation for free logic; some, for example, find a basis for free logic in the theory of attribution,[6] others believe the correct foundation for mathematical intuitionism requires a free logic, and still others think the theory of partial functions and the theory of definition are best founded on free logic.[7]

II. THE CHARACTER OF FREE LOGIC

The expression 'free logic' is an abbreviation for the phrase 'free of existence assumptions with respect to its terms, general and *singular*'. The expressions 'singular term' and 'general term' are used here in the contemporary way. Quine has put the distinction this way. A *general term* is one true of each object or pair of objects or triple of objects, and so on, if any, in a given class; a *singular term* is one which purports to refer to just one object.[8]

The following examples may be helpful. General terms are expressions such as 'man', 'talaria', 'greater than', 'brakeless trains', 'unicorn', 'satellite of the earth', and 'between California and the deep blue sea'. Notice that some of these expressions, for example, the expressions 'unicorn' and 'talaria', are true of no existing things. This is the reason for the words 'if any' in the definition of 'general term'. Singular terms are expressions such as 'The premier of Austria in 1980', 'suavity', 'being notable', '1', 'the satellite of the earth' and so on, and also expressions that do not refer to existent objects

---

[6] E.g. Scales, *Attribution and Existence*.

[7] Carl Posy, 'Free IPC is a Natural Logic', forthcoming in *Topoi*. See also the last chapter of the book by van Fraassen and Lambert entitled *Derivation and Counter example*. Finally see the chapter on definition in P. Suppes, *Introduction to Logic*, Van Nostrand, New York, 1957.

[8] *Word and Object*, p. 96.

such as 'Vulcan', 'Heimdal', 'The man born simultaneously of nine sibling jotun maidens', and 'Potsdorf'.[9]

The explanation of the phrase 'logic free of existence assumptions with respect to its terms, general and singular', then, is this: it means 'a logic in which quantificational phrases have existential import and there are no statements such that they are logically true only if it is true that G exists for all general terms G or it is true that s exists for all singular terms s'. It is this explanation that *defines* the expression 'free logic'.

For some perspective on the explanation, consider, first, a logic *not* free of existence assumptions with respect to its *general* terms, for instance a logic including the statement

(10) If all men are mortal, then there exist men that are mortal

as logically true. Notice that the statement 'Round squares exist' is false, and if the general terms 'men' and 'mortal' are replaced by the general term 'round squares', the resulting statement

(11) If all round squares are round squares, then there exist round squares that are round squares

is not true. To preserve the logical truth of the original statement, (10), then, the general term 'round squares' must not be allowed to replace the general terms 'men' and 'mortal' in the specimen statement, and generally no general term falsifying the condition 'G exists' can be allowed to replace the general terms 'men' and 'mortal' in the statement. So the logic containing the specimen statement (10) among its logical truths cannot be free of existence assumptions with respect to its general terms. Why? Because there are statements in that logic – (10), for example – that will not be logically true unless it is true that G exists for any general term G.

---

[9] The above examples are all *constants*, but in most formulations of elementary logic there occur individual variables, such as the letters 'x', 'y', and 'z', and in some others also property variables such as the letters 'P', 'Q', 'R'. They, too, are usually treated as a species of singular terms; they are *variable singular terms*.

Now consider a logic which is not free of existence assumptions with respect to its *singular* terms. In particular, consider one in which the statement

(12) There exists something that is identical with Carter

is logically true. Notice that the statement 'Pegasus exists' is false, and that if the singular term 'Pegasus' is put in the place of the singular term 'Carter' in the previous statement, the result is the untrue statement (5),

There exists something that is identical with Pegasus.

To preserve the logical truth of (12), then, the singular term 'Pegasus' must not be allowed to replace the word 'Carter' in the specimen statement (12), and generally no singular term that falsifies the condition '*s* exists' can be allowed to replace the singular term 'Carter' in (12). So a logic containing the specimen statement (12) among its logical truths is *not* free of existence assumptions with respect to its singular terms. Why? Because, again, there are statements in it that will not be logically true unless it is true that *s* exists, for any singular term *s*.

Logics that are free from existence assumptions with respect to their singular terms are now in plentiful supply, including apparently some versions of Lesniewski's 'ontology',[10] developed during the 1930s. There is an important implication of the preceding remarks to which attention should be drawn. As suggested a moment ago, in a free logic with identity, the statement (6),

There exists something identical with Pegasus,

is not true. On the other hand, the statement

(13) For every existing object there exists something identical with it

is logically true – hence true – in free logics with identity. It follows that the logical principle known as specification, that is, roughly, the principle that

---

[10] See Karel Lambert and Thomas Scharle, 'A Translation Theorem for Two Systems of Free Logic', *Logique et Analyse*, 40 (1967), pp. 328–41.

(14) If every existing thing x, ... x ... then ... s ...
where s is a singular term

or the corresponding rule called *universal instantiation*, that is, roughly, the rule that

(15) *Every existing thing* x, ... x ... where s is a singular term;
... s ...

is rejected in free logic. Similar examples sustain the rejection of the principle of particularization, that is, roughly, the principle that

(16) If ... s ... then there exists something x, ... x ...
where s is a singular term,

and the corresponding rule of *existential generalization*, that is, roughly, the rule that

(17) ... s ..., where s is a singular term;
There exists something x, ... x ...

I have described, in the barest outlines, what a free logic is. Since there are misunderstandings and confusions about it, some pretty well ingrained, let us turn to what free logic is not. The following comments should make more vivid this particular specimen in what Russell would have called 'our logical zoo'.

Some people have thought free logic to be terribly presumptuous, that no logic is free of all 'presuppositions.' This objection no doubt derives from the unfortunate inclination of some logicians, especially during the formative years of the subject, to refer to free logic as 'presupposition-free logic'. Still it is difficult to understand how this objection could ever have had any credibility except to those whose inflexibility matches the Gnat's in *Alice in Wonderland*.[11] For it is very clear even from

---

[11] It was the Gnat who exclaimed, 'What's the use of their having names if they won't answer to them?'

the most superficial inspection of 'presupposition-free logic'
that the presuppositions of concern to the free logician are
existence 'presuppositions', and those only.

What is an example of a logical 'presupposition' not at issue
in free logic? An instance is the 'presupposition' that the
inference patterns of both standard and free logic require in-
variability in the senses of expressions occurring more than
once in an argument. It is because of this precondition, for
example, that the argument

> Everything is such that if it is a nut then it grows on trees.
> Something that is a nut has threads;
> So, something that has threads grows on trees

is not accepted as evidence of the nonvalid character of the
inference pattern

> Everything is such that if it is (an) F then it is (a) G.
> Something that is (an) F has H;
> So, something that has H (is) G,

despite the apparent truth of the premises and the falsity of the
conclusion. Indeed, the example argument is an instance of
what is traditionally called an equivocation, an argument that
masquerades as a counterexample by virtue of a word or
phrase – in this case the word 'nut' – having different senses at
different occurrences in the argument. When the word is given
the same sense throughout the counterexample evaporates
because one or the other of the premises will turn out false.

A second misunderstanding about free logic concerns the
'empty world'. Long ago Russell complained about the impure
character of classical logical truths such as

> (18) If every existent is an oddity then there exists an
> oddity,

and

> (19) There exist objects identical with themselves.

According to Russell these statements are false if there are no objects. But, he thought, whether there are any objects at all, and how many there are, are matters of fact. So holding statements (18) and (19) to be logical truths seemed to him to compromise the idea of logical truth as not dependent on matters of fact, a conception he himself encouraged. Now what should be noticed is that one can reject, say, the principle of specification, a characteristic feature of free logics, and consistently hold that the statements (18) and (19) are logically true. To see this, imagine the world to contain as its sole existing object the renowned early twentieth-century logician Mary Caulkins. She is an excellent choice because, legend has it, she was a Solipsist.[12] Notice, first, that the way the principle of specification was disproved earlier still works; the statement (13),

> Every existent object is such that there exists something identical with it,

is true of the imagined world, but the statement (6),

> There exists something identical with Pegasus,

is not. Notice, second, that because of Mary Caulkins the statements (18) and (19) do not fail. The matter can be summed up in this way. If the world were empty then, of course, all singular terms would fail to refer; but if the world had things in it, it might still be the case that not any of them would be specified by a singular term such as 'Pegasus'.

A free logic recognizing the empty world is, to be sure, easy to develop. A free logic making room for the empty world is conventionally called a *universally free logic*.[13] But, the point is, one might legitimately believe in a theory of singular inference that allows singular terms referring to no existing object while nevertheless not sharing Russell's sentiments about the logic

---

[12] She is also alleged to be responsible for a remarkable self-indicting response to a friend who met her as she was about to board a ship for England. 'Where are you going, Mary?' he asked. 'To a Solipsist convention in London,' she replied.

[13] See, for example, the formulation of Robert Meyer and Karel Lambert, 'Universally Free Logic and Standard Quantification Theory', *Journal of Symbolic Logic*, 38 (1968), pp. 8–26.

impurity of statements (18) and (19). So there is more than one kind of existence assumption, and free logic has to do only with one of them.

A third misunderstanding about free logic concerns its relation to the conventional logic of predicates. Many philosophers – perhaps most – have the impression that free logic is an alteration of conventional predicate logic in the sense that though all the principles of free logic are conventionally acceptable, some conventional principles are not acceptable to the free logician. But free logic need not be considered an alternative to classical predicate logic. Interested persons can hardly be blamed for the present misunderstanding when the status of the theory *vis à vis* conventional predicate logic was not always clearly perceived by the founders of the subject.

The issue concerns exactly what conventional predicate logic is. Thus, suppose conventional predicate logic is formulated as Quine formulates it in *Word and Object*. There the primitive vocabulary contains no constant singular terms, though it does contain variable singular terms; that is, symbols such as 'x', 'y', 'z', and so on, that must always represent actual objects. These variables are not thought of as stand-ins for constant singular terms by Quine in logical formula such as 'Fx'. So the traditional logical principles of specification and particularization can and do hold for the free variables.

The only nonlogical constants in this version are predicates, that is, words and phrases like 'suave' and 'great economic brain'. From this standpoint no free logician challenges the conventional logic of predicates. So when constant singular terms such as 'Pegasus' and 'Carter' are added to the vocabulary, the resulting logic – which is free because, as shown earlier, the principle of specification fails for singular terms such as 'Pegasus' – the resulting logic is an *extension* of classical predicate logic rather than an alteration of it.[14]

---

[14] The treatment, in other words, is quite analogous to those formulations of modal statement logic that simply add principles and rules for the expression 'it is necessary that' to conventional statement logic.

Failure to perceive this sort of treatment of free logic, exemplified by van Fraassen and Lambert, for example, in *Derivation and Counterexample*, flaws Susan Haack's discussion of free logic as an alternative to classical logic in her book, *Deviant Logic*.[15] Free logic, as a matter of fact, *can* be understood as an alternative to conventional predicate logic even when it contains no singular terms but variables. If you imagine the free variables functioning in part as stand-ins for singular term constants, then, indeed, some of the free variables may sometimes name no actual object. So, as in the case of expressions such as 'Pegasus', specification fails under this semantic policy.[16] Sometimes it is useful to think of free logic as an extension of conventional predicate logic, because it helps to *isolate* questions of singular inference. This strategy provides a clear view of the distinctive differences between free logic and the Frege and Russell theories of singular inference.

Since the subject of semantics has now been raised, this is the appropriate place to deal with another common misunderstanding about free logic. Opinion is about equally divided among non specialists that free logicians are either all Russellians or all non-Russellians. Here, non-Russellians are treated as those who accept nonexistents, and Russellians as those who deny them.

The current misunderstanding is probably a product of the place where one meets a free logic first. For instance, if one's first exposure is to a development like that in Tyler Burge's essay 'Truth and Singular Terms', the lack of an 'outer domain' in the description of the models for his system, or of a complete interpretation function for the singular terms, may cause one to jump to the conclusion that free logic is inspired by a Russellian ontic disposition coupled with a rejection of Russell's theory of logical form. On the other hand, if one's initial exposure is to a paper like that of Leblanc and Thomason, 'Completeness Theorems for Presupposition Free

---

[15] Cambridge University Press, Cambridge, 1974.
[16] I actually followed this policy in my 1963 paper, 'Existential Import Revisited', *Notre Dame Journal of Formal Logic*, 4 (1963), pp. 288–92; so have many others.

Logics',[17] replete as it is with 'outer domains' and complete interpretation functions for singular terms one may jump to the conclusion that free logic is non-Russellian. But these two extreme conclusions are unwarranted. For example, in the above-mentioned paper by Meyer and Lambert, 'Universally Free Logic and Standard Quantification Theory', there is an explicit denial of non-Russellianism despite 'outer domains'; our outer domains are conceived as a set of expressions. Free logic, thus, does not imply, nor should it be saddled with, any particular ontological inclination. So far as ontic proclivities are concerned free logic is truly free.

In the same vein, consider a slogan almost synonymous with free logic in the minds of many, namely that free logic is the logic of irreferential singular terms. I alluded to this matter at the end of Chapter 2. The slogan is not so much a misunderstanding as it is a misleading way of expressing what is true about free logic. The issue concerns the exact meaning of the word 'irreferential'– or its fellows, the words 'nondenoting', 'empty', 'vacuous', etc. as they apply to singular terms. Most people currently use the expression 'irreferential' as synonymous with 'does not refer to an existent object'. This usage would not be at all confusing were it not for the penchant of many free logicians, following Russell, to equate the objects with the existent objects. But there are free logicians of a distinctly non-Russellian inclination who, rejecting the equation of the objects with the existents, thus are left apparently asserting that the word 'Heimdal' is irreferential because it refers to no existent but nevertheless is referential because it also refers to the non-existent object whose birth was nine times as virginal as Christ's. This confusing talk of words and phrases that are both 'referential' in one sense and 'irreferential' in another sense should simply be abandoned. The expression 'irreferential' and its synonyms should be reserved to mean 'does not refer to anything' – minus the qualifier 'existent'. A free logician whose ontic proclivities are not Russellian, then, is simply mischaracterized as one who admits no irreferential singular terms in his logical language. Not that there aren't those (such as Terence Parsons in *Nonexistent Objects*) who argue for the plausibility of nonexistent objects but who also deny that every singular term refers.

Another misunderstanding is the belief that free logic is somehow committed to the doctrine that existence is a predicate. This belief stems no doubt from the fact that many versions of free logic employ a primitive or defined symbol 'E' – more often 'E!' – as the formal representative of the English word 'exists' or other natural language equivalents of the English word – for example *existiert* in German. Nevertheless the belief is mistaken.

In the first place, if one understands the traditional doctrine to concern nonlinguistic *things* (namely, properties) rather than words – and I think this is the proper construal – it is not at all clear that the occurrence of 'E' in the language of free logic *even as a primitive predicate* commits one to the position that existence is a property of individuals. In fact in these systems of free logic, it is not at all clear that existence is a property of *anything*, be it a property of properties, or of propositional functions, or anything else. The point here is not the Quineian one that the expression 'E' is a general term and general terms don't *refer*, and so don't refer to properties. Rather the point is that, even granted that general terms stand for things (though not in the sense names stand for things), and also are true of things and have extensions, the primitive symbol 'E' need not, and may not in fact, stand for properties of anything in some developments of free logic. Thus, for example, Leonard, in his foundational essay, 'The Logic of Existence,'[18] allows only one of the symbols 'E', or its complement 'Ē' ('is nonexistent'), to stand for a property. But in a free logic *even in principle* it is no more necessary for any given general term to stand for something than it is for any given singular term to refer to actual things – or to anything at all for that matter.

In the second place, if the traditional doctrine that existence is not a predicate is understood in the weak sense, that is, as

[18] *Philosophical Studies*, 7 (1956), pp. 49–64.

the doctrine that the word 'existence' does not properly belong to the logical category of predicates, then even in this sense free logic does not require that existence be treated as a predicate. On the one hand, those who introduce the symbol 'E' contextually – understood as short for existence – do not always construe the symbol as a predicate, as Russell does in his theory of definite descriptions. On the other hand, there are developments of free logic that contain no symbol at all for 'exists', nor even envisage paraphrases into the formal object language of natural language sentences containing that word as a part.

The systematization of Brian Skyrms[19] is a case in point. Nor does any of this mean the earlier informal characterization of free logic suffers; that characterization, in effect, appeals to statements containing the word 'exists' without taking a position on the logical form of such statements or the category of logical grammar to which the word 'exists' belongs. Of course, none of this rules out the possibility that 'E' (or 'exists') can be explicitly introduced as an expression in the linguistic category of predicate in a free logic.

A final misunderstanding concerns the way in which quantificational expressions such as 'Something' are understood in free logic. As the definition of free logic some pages back makes clear, 'Something' has existential force, the force of 'There exists'. Some have thought that the valid inference patterns and laws of standard symbolic logic can be maintained consistent with the tenets of free logic by simply switching from the 'referential' (or 'objectual') interpretation to the substitutional interpretation. But this is mistaken. One can give substitutional accounts of the quantifiers which conform to the demands of free logic and substitutional accounts which do not. For example, the interpretation 'Something x is such that x is blue' is true just in case the result of replacing 'x' in 'x is blue' by a name referring or a name not referring to an existent' is true, is substitutional but is not acceptable to the

---

[19] See, for example, his formulation in 'Supervaluations: Identity, Existence and Individual Concepts'.

free logician. If the phrase 'or not referring to an existent' is deleted from the above interpretation principle, one still has a substitutional interpretation of 'Something', and an interpretation acceptable to free logicians. The effect of the deletion is to give the quantificational expression 'Something' existential force.

The present misunderstanding derives from a misreading of the goal of free logics. Free logics are aimed at providing different resolutions to problems involving inferences containing singular terms that refer to no existent, but within the conventional understanding of the quantifiers. For them, the inference pattern called existential generalization means exactly what the classical logician says it does, but fails when constant singular terms referring to no actual thing are considered. In fact, the contrasting free logic approach to what amounts to the substitutional approach (reflected in the original interpretation principle enunciated above) was outlined by me against Lejewski in 1965.[20]

III. INDEPENDENCE AND FREE LOGIC

In Chapter 3 it was argued that the principle of independence yields the principle that a predication does not imply the being of the object (or objects) purported to be referred to by its constituent singular term (or terms). So where 'G' is a 1-place general term, say 'rotates', and 's' is a singular term, say 'Vulcan', the principle of independence implies that the argument

Gs;
So, s has being

is invalid. And the same would hold, of course, where 'G' is 'spherical', and 's' is 'the spheroid which is such that it is not a spheroid'.

Simple predications – predications with simple general

---

[20] Karel Lambert, 'On Logic and Existence', *Notre Dame Journal of Formal Logic*, 6 (1965), pp. 135–41.

terms – are the main topic of concern here; different kinds of free logic result from beliefs or policies about the truth-values, if any, that ought to be accorded to simple predications. Because the principle of abstraction has no untoward consequences where simple predications are the concern, we can concentrate on simple statements themselves. For example, consider the 2-place general term 'is identical with'. The simple statements will include statements such as 'Heimdal is identical with Heimdal', 'Heimdal is identical with Voltaire', 'Heimdal is identical with Vulcan', 'Potsdorf is identical with Salzburg', 'The spheroid which is such that it is not a spheroid is identical with The spheroid which is such that it is not a spheroid', and so on. Now some free logicians think all the examples of simple statements are false, in the spirit of Russell. A free logic so motivated is a *negative free logic*.[21]

Other free logics count at least the statements 'The spheroid which is such that it is not a spheroid is identical with the spheroid which is such that it is not a spheroid' and 'Heimdal is identical with Heimdal' true, and some, perhaps in the spirit of Frege's attitude towards scientific language, even count *any* simple statement containing only singular terms that do not refer to existents true. Free logics of this sort are *positive free logics*.[22]

Finally, there are free logicians who think all the examples of simple identity statements are truth-valueless, in the spirit of Frege's attitude toward colloquial discourse. Free logics counting all simple statements containing at least one singular term that does not refer to an existent truth-valueless (except, of course, simple statements of the form '*s* exists', where '*s*' does not refer to an existent) are *neuter free logics*.[23]

Different opinions or convictions about the truth-values of simple predications containing singular terms that do not refer to any existing objects help determine which statements are

---

[21] Burge, 'Truth and Singular Terms'.
[22] Meyer and Lambert, 'Universally Free Logic and Standard Quantification Theory'.
[23] Skyrms, 'Supervaluations: Identity, Existence and Individual Concepts'.

(or are not) logically true and which inferences are (or are not) valid. To illustrate, consider the simple statement, familiar from earlier chapters,

> (20) The spheroid which is such that it is not a spheroid is identical with the spheroid which is such that it is not a spheroid.

This statement is a predication in anyone's free logic despite differences in the core principle (hence in the theory) of predication. Negative free logicians, as just announced, regard (20) as false. It follows immediately that it is not logically true. More importantly, according falsehood to (20) sustains the inferential conviction of negative free logicians that if '*Gs*' is a simple predication, the inference to '*s* has being' is fully warranted, on the ground, say, that nothing can have no attributes. This inferential conviction, of course, is directly at odds with the principle of independence because that principle entails unprovisionally the conviction that if '*Gs*' is a simple predication, then it simply does not follow that '*s* has being'. The discussion can be inverted; belief in the falsity of (20) can be seen as a consequence of the falsity of

> (21) The spheroid which is such that it is not a spheroid has being

and the inferential conviction that simple predications imply the being of their purported referents. Usually this is the way discussion of the truth-value of (20) evolves.

Turn now to the positive free logician. For him, (20) is true – indeed logically true – perhaps 'by virtue of meaning alone'. So it would be impossible for this brand of free logician, in the face of the falsity of (21), to hold the inferential conviction of the negative free logician just examined; rather the inference from '*Gs*' to '*s* has being' is invalid. Hence, in positive free logic the principle that predications do not imply the being of their purported referents is sustained. So it must be the case, given the falsity of (21), that some predications containing the singular term 'the spheroid which is such that it is not a spheroid' are true (though it doesn't follow from this inferential conviction that (20) *itself must* be true – as noted in the last chapter). To sum up, in positive free logics, in contrast to negative free logics, the predicational cousin of the principle of independence holds. Indeed, it is entailed by positive free logic, and in the debate among free logicians concerning the 'correct' free logic, it would probably be regarded as its *leading principle*.

Given that the principle of independence affects one's theory of predication, it is clear that one of the fundamental cleavages between negative and positive free logics is their differing views about predication. This matter arose in the preceding chapter in the long first footnote (p. 69). There, Richard Grandy, a positive free logician, was quoted as attributing the difference between his formulation of free logic and the formulation of Tyler Burge, a negative free logician, to a fundamental disagreement about 'the concept of predication'. But what exactly does this come to? The question is pivotal because the adversaries disagree both about their core principles of predication and about the acceptability of the classical constraint – at least in the restricted form that a statement having the form of a simple predication implies the being of its purported referent(s). Grandy believes in the core principle CT; for him the truth of a predication depends on whether the constituent general term is true of the object(s) specified by the singular term(s); and similarly for the falsity of a predication. At the core, he is a traditionalist. But he rejects the traditional constraint; he accepts the predicational cousin of the principle of independence, that the being of the purported referents of a predication does not follow from the fact that a statement has the form of a predication. (He would surely accept the principle of independence in the strict sense were his language extended to allow statements such as 'Object *s* has *some* properties.' Without quantification over properties, or some equivalent, the principle of independence cannot be expressed.)

Burge, on the other hand, adopts the core principle $C\overline{T}$, the principle that the truth-value of a predication depends on the constituent general term being true (or false) of the referent(s) of the constituent singular term(s) *were* these singular terms to refer. So, at the core, Burge is a nontraditionalist. But he accepts the traditional constraint that the purported referents of a predication have being.

The precise content of Grandy's conviction about the underlying source of disagreement between free logicians, be they negative, positive or neuter, is this. The underlying theories of predication differ *essentially* on the acceptability of the traditional constraint; the character of the core principle of predication is an *inessential* difference. If this is correct, as will shortly be argued, then the philosophical difference of importance between free logicians has to do with the principle of independence; for it entails the falsity of the traditional constraint. Whatever philosophical support it has, then, transfers to positive free logic as the most adequate version of free logic. And thus the connection between the Mally–Meinong doctrine and the most recent of theories of singular inference, the free logic tradition emerges. That principle amounts to a fundamental desideratum in the general question: what is the correct theory of singular inference?

Now to the argument that it is not the core of the theory of predication underlying a free logic that is essential to the truth-values of the simple predications, but instead the traditional constraint. Consider one of the formulations of free logic discussed earlier, the version van Fraassen and I develop in our book, *Derivation and Counterexample*. Like Grandy's formulation, it is a positive free logic, but its semantical underpinning and, as one might expect, its core principle of predication, is very different. In Grandy's development every singular term refers to some object but only some of them refer to existents. Grandy admits an 'outer domain' of virtual objects, as the model structures he delineates make clear. In the development presented by van Fraassen and me, an outer domain of objects of any kind is specifically eschewed. Like Burge, we take singular terms like 'Vulcan', 'Heimdal', and

'The spheroid which is such that it is not a spheroid' to be irreferential. And, indeed, the core principle of predication in our formulation in *Derivation and Counterexample* is exactly like that of Tyler Burge; we adopt, in other words, $C\overline{T}$, *contra* Grandy. Nevertheless, like Grandy, we espouse the principle that the purported referents of a predication need not have being. For, in our development, the predicational statement (20),

> The spheroid which is such that it is not a spheroid is identical with the spheroid which is such that it is not a spheroid

is true, even though the constituent singular term 'The spheroid which is such that it is not a spheroid' is irreferential. This is accomplished by the introduction of the notion of a story to be used in determining the truth-value of statements such as those above, and a condition on stories is that all statements of the form

> s is identical with s

are contained in them. (The rough idea is that if a statement contains at least one irreferential singular term, then it is true just in case it is in the story.)

It should be clear, then, that what brings about the difference in truth-value policies toward simple predications, hence between positive and negative free logics, concerns not the predicational core of those theories, but rather the predicational constraint. It is because the principle of independence concerns the constraints on the theory of predication that it is crucial in the truth-value policies of Burge, on the one hand, and Grandy, and van Fraassen and me, on the other hand.

If it is now clear how the same core principle of predication is consistent with different policies concerning the truth-values of simple predications, it should be equally clear that different core principles of predication in and of themselves need not necessarily occasion different truth-value verdicts concerning simple predications. This is perhaps most dramatically seen in the comparison of Russell's theory of singular inference with that of Scales and Burge. They differ at the core, but assign the same truth-values to all simple predications, indeed to all predications. It is also true that a free logician can be utterly traditional at the predicational core, but positive in truth-value policy; on the other hand, he can also be quite non-traditional in his theory of predication, yet positive in his truth-value verdicts. This should not be altogether unexpected. Reflection on the fact established in Chapter 3 that the principle of independence does not entail a world of nonbeings, and thus does not encourage open-armed acceptance of the core of the traditional theory of predication, should explain why. It is possible, after all, to agree with leading Meinongian principles while not sharing his world view. Such evidently is the case for those positive free logicians who share Russell's robust sense of reality, but who find his sense of truth and logical form far more anemic when compared with Meinong's.

The connections between free logic, irreferential singular terms, and Meinongian ontology and principles can be summarized briefly. First, it does not follow that acceptance of a free logic commits one to a belief in irreferential singular terms. But that does not mean one is thereby a Meinongian. The belief that 'Heimdal' or 'Vulcan' refer, but to nonexistents, does not mean the bearers of those names are objects in the Meinongian sense because they may merely be 'virtual objects' in Scott's sense. On the other hand, it does not follow that one who believes in irreferential singular terms is thereby committed to a free logic. Terence Parsons, for example, thinks the singular term 'Vulcan', in some uses, is irreferential, but, like Meinong and unlike free logicians, he does not always attach existential force to the quantificational expressions 'There is' and 'Everything'.[24] There is, therefore, no hard and fast association between free logic and the logic of irreferential singular terms, though to be sure one of the main motivations behind some developments of free logic lies in the belief that some singular terms are irreferential.

[24] See his *Nonexistent Objects*.

Though no free logician shares Meinong's world picture, some certainly share the inferential conviction expressed in his principle of independence. Indeed, it is perhaps the major distinguishing principle in the partitioning of free logics, and it can play its part irrespective of one's belief in the referential status of 'Vulcan' or 'the spheroid which is such that it is not a spheroid'.

6

INDEPENDENCE VINDICATED

Previous chapters have been devoted to the explanation and implications of the principle of independence derived from Meinong. The implications studied were of two sorts – those having to do with the theory of predication and those having to do with logics free of existence assumptions with respect to their general and singular terms. Yet even this small subset of the implications of the principle of independence shows the importance of that principle in the subject matters it touches. It is a matter of no little moment what the 'best' theory of singular inference is, and in this regard the principle of independence is a dominant consideration. The question, then, is whether the principle of independence is true. The final chapter addresses this topic.

The direct topic of concern in this chapter is the principle of which the following is a special case:

Gs;
So, s has being

is *invalid*. Most of the discussion from here on proceeds by way of this special case.

It will be valuable to review the connections – or rather the lack of them – between the principle of predication just outlined and various principles and conceptions discussed in previous pages. In the first place, the principle in question neither implies nor is implied by the assertion that the constituent singular terms of a predication are referential. The same holds also as far as the irreferentiality of the constituent singular terms is concerned. Consider, for example, the inference

Pegasus flies;
So, Pegasus has being.

From the supposed fact that the statement

Pegasus flies

is true, and the statement

Pegasus has being

is false, a consequence of the supposed invalidity of the argument of which the former is the premise and the latter the conclusion, nothing can be inferred about the referring status of 'Pegasus'. Meinong would hold that 'Pegasus' indeed is referential, and many free logicians would hold it to be irreferential. But the reasons for either position lie in the main in other parts of the respective theories.

In the second place, and closely related to the observation just made, the principle of predication in question does not imply, nor is it implied by, a particular core principle of predication – at least it does not imply, nor is it implied by, any of the core principles touched on in the previous chapters. The upshot of these two observations is clear enough; whatever the ultimate verdict about the referential status of a singular term such as 'Pegasus', or about the various core principles of predication, nothing follows from those verdicts alone about the correctness of the principle that the purported referents of the singular terms of a predication need have no being, and thus about the correctness of its intimate cousin, the principle of independence. The general point that again emerges is that there is little connection between belief in what there is (or isn't) and the principle of independence.

Whatever the ultimate decision on Meinong's conviction that the inference

The spheroid which is such that it is not a spheroid is spherical;
So, the spheroid which is such that it is not a spheroid has being

is invalid, he had plenty of other examples at hand to make his point. Doubtless, he would have regarded the inferences

Pegasus flies;
So, Pegasus has being

and

Vulcan is Vulcan;
So, Vulcan has being

as invalid. (Vulcan, here, is the purported but beingless planet, not the god.) Opponents of Meinong's view fix on one and/or another of three features of the predicational cousin of the Meinong–Mally principle of independence: (a) that, for example, the statements

Pegasus has being

and

Vulcan has being

are false; (b) that, for example, the statements

Pegasus flies

and

Vulcan is Vulcan

are predications; and (c) that, for example, the two immediately preceding statements are true. To say that 'Pegasus flies' or 'Vulcan is Vulcan' are predications does not necessarily commit one to a particular *theory* of predication. The belief might be merely a preanalytical conviction; it would amount to the belief that the truth-value of the statement thought to be a predication is dependent on some relation between constituent general term and constituent singular terms in some or all circumstances.

II. ARGUMENTS AGAINST INDEPENDENCE

Complaints against the invalidity of an inference of the form

$Gs;$
So, s has being,

fixing particularly on the falsehood of the conclusion, are rare but not unknown. There is, for example, the exception provided by Russell in *The Principles of Mathematics*.[1] There he considered statements such as

(1) Vulcan is Vulcan

to be legitimate instances of the form

(2) Gs,

hence genuine predications. He also took them to be true. Yet the statement

(3) Vulcan has being

he counted true. Indeed, he thought *any* appropriate instance of

(4) s has being

incontrovertibly true. The evidence for this last claim is contained in remarks about being toward the end of his great work, remarks reminiscent of certain passages in Plato's *Sophist*:

Being is that which belongs to every conceivable, to every possible object of thought – in short to everything that can possibly occur in any proposition, true or false, and to all such propositions themselves. Being belongs to whatever can be counted. If A be any term that can be counted as one, it is plain that A is something, and therefore that A is. 'A is not' must always be either false or meaningless. For if A were nothing, it could not be said not to be; 'A is not' implies

[1] The University Press, Cambridge, 1903.

that there is a term A whose being is denied, and hence that whatever A may be, it certainly is. Numbers, the Homeric gods, relations, chimeras and four-dimensional spaces all have being, for if they were not entities of a kind, we could make no propositions about them. Thus being is a general attribute of everything, and to mention anything is to show that it is.[2]

A sketch of the key part of Russell's argument for the truth of all instances of (4), hence of (3), recast into the parlance of this book, is as follows. The statement in (4),

Vulcan has being,

is true because the expression 'Vulcan', being significant, stands for an object, something which 'can be counted as one', and nothing can be counted as one unless it has being.

Russell's argument for the truth of any instance of (4), hence of (3), is now largely discredited. Russell himself helped to bring about this state of affairs. He reported in the second edition of *The Principles of Mathematics*[3] that he had come to believe that significant expressions need not stand for objects ('terms', in the language of the *Principles*), and in particular that an expression such as 'Vulcan' need not, and does not, refer to an object. With the exception of unrepentant Meinongians, the majority of analytic philosophers agree. So the first premise of Russell's earlier argument for the truth of all instances of (4), hence, in particular, of (3), is suspect, and thus the soundness of that argument is questionable.

Nor is the second premise of his argument unobjectionable. As explained earlier in this book, Meinong protested against the assertion that nothing can be an object unless it has being. Later work provides considerable support for Meinong's conviction if not for his reasons. For example, Terence Parsons' *Nonexistent Objects* has provided a clear characterization of something analogous to the Meinongian conception of an object, and it is easily verifiable in that semantic account that not all objects have being. So given that Meinongian objects

---

[2] *Ibid.*, p. 449.
[3] Norton, New York, 1938; p. x.

are at least objects in the sense of things 'countable as one' – and they are – there is again reason to suspect another premise in Russell's argument, and thus again the soundness of his argument.

Russell's argument aside, what is the worth of his remark that 'A is' must be true, and 'A is not' must be either meaningless or false? ('A', presumably, can be replaced by any and only a singular term.) It seems clear that 'A is' simply means 'A has being', but the question is, what does Russell intend by *that*? It is unlikely that he meant by 'being' what Meinong meant by 'object'. He had his own equivalent expression for 'object', namely, the expression 'term', and he certainly didn't think the assertion 'Nothing can be a term unless it has being' tautological. It is quite unlikely, therefore, that the issue between Meinong and Russell over the nature of objects is merely verbal. Borrowing Meinong's verb cognate for the noun 'being' – the word 'subsists' – Russell's intention, I think, is expressed by the locution 'There subsists something (x, such that x is) identical with A'. Now statements of identity are true just in case the singular terms flanking the expression of identity refer to the same thing. For example,

(5) Lincoln is identical with The Great Emancipator

is true because 'Lincoln' and 'The Great Emancipator' refer to the same thing – the writer of *The Gettysburg Address*. So long as 'A' is assumed to be a constant or a variable singular term, Russell's early conviction that

(6) There subsists something (x, such that x is) identical with A

must be true is open to serious question.

There are two cases. Suppose 'A' is replaced by a referential singular term. Then, as noted above, there are semantic developments in which 'A' can specify a nonsubsistent object. But then no matter what subsistent 'x' in 'x is identical with A' specifies, and it must specify one, 'x' and 'A', as imagined above, will have different referents, and 'x is identical with A' will be false for all possible referents of '*x*'. So (6) would be false, under the imagined referent of A. So, where 'A' is referential, there is no question of necessity, because (6) could be false. Now suppose 'A' is replaced by an irreferential singular term. Then, clearly 'A' would never refer to what '*x*' refers to, since '*x*' always refers to a subsistent. Again, (6) turns out to be false, under the imagined conditions. Thus, it may be concluded again, and finally, that

(7) A is

is not necessarily true, and, indeed, can be factually false. Such is the case, for example, with

(8) Vulcan is,

against the Russell of the *Principles*.

Next, those who defend the validity of

Gs;
So, *s* has being

often respond to alleged infractions such as

Vulcan is Vulcan;
So, Vulcan has being

by denying that (1),

Vulcan is Vulcan,

has the form of a predication, and hence by denying that the inference above of which (1) is the premise has the appropriate form to be a counterexample to

Gs;
So, *s* has being.

This maneuver to sustain the validity of the inference pattern in question, and hence ultimately the rejection of the principle of independence, is by far the most popular and widespread. The inspiration, again, is Russell, but not the Russell of *The Principles of Mathematics*. It is the Russell of 1905 and always thereafter; it is the Russell emerging in that profound and dramatic study, 'On Denoting'. In that essay, Russell introduces for the first time, and sketchily, his theory of definite descriptions. In fact, in 'On Denoting', that theory is but a special case of his more general theory of denoting expressions, a topic which had occupied him in *The Principles of Mathematics* but which receives a radically different treatment in his 1905 paper. The leading principle of that essay is the injunction to beware of the grammatical appearances because they are misleading indicators of logical form.

Many years later, in a letter to Quine, Russell emphasized that philosophical considerations were among the main motivations behind his famous theory of descriptions, and in particular, Meinong's theory of objects. He wrote:

> In reading you I was struck by the fact that, in my work, I was always being influenced by extraneous philosphical considerations. Take e.g., descriptions. I was interested in 'Scott is the author of *Waverley*', and not only in the descriptive functions of PM [*Principia Mathematica*]. If you look up Meinong's work, you will see the sort of fallacies I wanted to avoid; the same applies to the ontological argument.[4]

What were the Meinongian fallacies of which Russell spoke? Essentially, they were arguments whose conclusions expressed information about certain beingless objects such as the round square and the present king of France. Because of these 'fallacies', Russell came to believe that there were not, and could not be, any beingless objects. He thought Meinong was forced into illicit claims about beingless objects by a wrong conception of the logical form of statements purporting to be about such objects. Later, in *Principia Mathematica*, he gave a general argument in favor of his conception of logical form and against Meinong's. The matter deserves much closer scrutiny.

One measure of a philosopher's profundity is the detection and demonstration of the importance of assumptions underlying doctrines that others take for granted, if they notice them

---

[4] *The Autobiography of Bertrand Russell, The Middle Years: 1914–1944* (Little, Brown, New York, 1969), p. 309.

at all. Russell himself is a case in point. It was he who brought attention to the importance of assumptions about logical form in the support offered by many of its proponents for absolute idealism. Consider, for example, the scathing attack on Hegel in the following passage.

Hegel's argument in this portion of his 'Logic' depends throughout upon confusing the 'is' of predication, as in 'Socrates is mortal', with the 'is' of identity, as in 'Socrates is the philosopher who drank the hemlock.' Owing to this confusion, he thinks that 'Socrates' and 'mortal' must be identical. Seeing that they are different, he does not infer, as others would, that there is a mistake somewhere, but that they exhibit 'identity in difference'. Again, Socrates is particular, 'mortal' is universal. Therefore, he says, since Socrates is mortal, it follows that the particular is the universal – taking the 'is' to be throughout expressive of identity. But to say 'the particular is the universal' is self-contradictory. Again Hegel does not suspect a mistake, but proceeds to synthesise particular and universal in the individual, or concrete universal. This is an example of how, for want of care at the start, vast and imposing systems of philosophy are built upon stupid and trivial confusions, which, but for the almost incredible fact that they are unintentional, one would be tempted to characterise as puns.[5]

And it was Russell again who urged the importance of the assumption that statements such as

(9) The round square is round

and

(10) The existent present king of France exists

have the logical form of predications in Meinong's belief in a world of beingless objects. Though he mentioned the matter in many places, the source most remembered is 'On Denoting', where he sought to show that Meinong's admission of the contradiction ensuing from acceptance of statements such as (9) and

[5] Bertrand Russell, *Our Knowledge of the External World*, p. 42.

(11) The round square is not round

was to be traced to Meinong's conviction that both (7) and (10) are predications (approximately in the sense of the core principle CT). He seems to have believed that the idea that expressions such as 'The round square' stand for objects, albeit beingless ones, inevitably leads to contradiction.[6] And he believed in the principle that the singular terms in a purported predication had to stand for objects if the predication were at all genuine.[7] Indeed, given classical logic, he is right if the core principle of predication is CT, as noted in Chapter 3. So, he seems to have thought (9) and (10) cannot be genuine predications after all.

But this sort of argument shows only that statements such as (9), and perhaps (10), are not genuine predications, not that *all* statements involving definite descriptions and yet other statements such as (1),

Vulcan is Vulcan,

are nonpredications. Many such statements are not only noncontradictory but also are *prima facie* true even though the grammatical subject is irreferential. Russell took care of this problem in *Principia Mathematica*. There he presented essentially an argument by cases that simple statements including definite descriptions are not predications because definite descriptions are not 'logical subjects'. Moreover, because 'Vulcan' is really a 'truncated description', according to the doctrine in 'On Denoting', it is also not a logical subject, and hence (1) fails to be a predication.

Russell's argument in *Principia Mathematica* that definite descriptions are not logical subjects (are 'incomplete symbols') may be summed up as follows.[8] Suppose a definite description

---

[6] Russell, *Logic and Knowledge*, (ed. Robert C. Marsh; Allen and Unwin, London, 1956), p. 54.

[7] *Ibid.*, p. 51.

[8] Whitehead and Russell, *Principia Mathematica* (2nd edn), pp. 66–7. The appropriate passages are:

Suppose we say: 'The round square does not exist.' It seems plain that this is a true proposition, yet we cannot regard it as denying the existence of a certain object

has a basis – 'so and so' in 'the so and so' – that is not true of exactly one existent, and suppose the description refers to some object. Then if the object exists, any statement of the form

(12) The so and so exists

would be true, contradicting the *fact* that no statement of the form of (12) is true. So no statement containing a definite description with an unfulfilled basis can be a predication, in the sense of the core principle CT, because no such definite description is a logical subject.

Consider next a definite description with a fulfilled basis – a basis true of exactly one existent. And suppose, again, it refers to some object (i.e., is a logical subject). Then it can enter into true identity statements containing a genuine logical subject on the other side of the identity. Thus if '*a*' is the logical subject,

(13) *a* is the so and so

can be true. Suppose it is. Now 'The so and so' can mean the same as '*a*' or mean something other than '*a*'. If the former, then (13) means the same as

(14) *a* is *a*,

'which it plainly does not'. If the latter, then (13) is false, which contradicts the hypothesis that it is true. So 'The so and so', though having a fulfilled basis, cannot be a logical subject, and thus no statement containing it can be a predication, in

called 'the round square.' For if there were such an object, it would exist: we cannot first assume that there is a certain object, and then proceed to deny that there is such an object. Whenever the grammatical subject of a proposition can be supposed not to exist without rendering the proposition meaningless, it is plain that the grammatical subject is not a proper name, i.e., not a name directly representing some object.

... Thus all phrases (other than propositions) containing the word *the* (in the singular) are incomplete symbols: they have a meaning in use, but not in isolation. For 'the author of Waverley' cannot mean the same as 'Scott,' or 'Scott is the author of Waverley' would mean the same as 'Scott is Scott,' which it plainly does not; nor can 'the author of Waverley' mean anything other than 'Scott', or 'Scott is the author of Waverley' would be false. Hence 'the author of Waverley' means nothing.

the sense of the core principle CT.

If not a predication, what form does (1),

Vulcan is Vulcan,

have? According to Russell, all simple statements containing definite descriptions are really existentially quantified statements. For example,

> (15) The planet causing the perturbations in Mercury's orbit is the planet causing the perturbations in Mercury's orbit

becomes

> (16) There exists exactly one thing which is a planet causing the perturbations in Mercury's orbit.

Since, for Russell, 'Vulcan' is convenient shorthand for 'The planet causing the perturbations in Mercury's orbit', the logical form of (1) is really the logical form of (16).

There are specific reasons why Russell's arguments that definite descriptions are not logical subjects fail. First, the argument that fulfilled definite descriptions are not logical subjects is equivocal. The word 'means' is ambiguous. It could mean 'have the same referent', which is needed to sustain the second premise, but falsifies the first premise. Or it could mean 'has the same meaning', which is needed to sustain the first premise, but falsifies the second premise. Second, the argument that unfulfilled descriptions are not logical subjects is quite dubious. It is highly debatable, as has been noted many times in previous pages, that to refer an unfulfilled definite description must specify an object having being (existence). Third, there are ample studies to show that Russell's (and Meinong's) belief that the admission of beingless objects necessarily leads to contradiction is wrong.[9] Hence a key component of his complaint against Meinong in 'On Denoting' is vitiated.

There are also more general reasons undercutting Russell's

---

[9] E.g. Parsons, *Nonexistent Objects*, p. 30.

arguments that definite descriptions are not logical subjects, be they explicit ('the author of *Waverley*') or truncated ('Vulcan'), and that statements containing them, therefore, are not predications. In the first place, Russell's attitude toward beingless objects is very different from his attitude toward classes (sets). In the latter case, his discovery that the class that bears his name – the Russell class (i.e., the class of all classes which are not members of themselves) – renders the naive theory of classes inconsistent, if presumed to exist, did not cause him to abandon the notion of classes. No indeed; rather it led him to alter some of the principles of the naive theory of classes. And thus the theory of types was born. Others have proposed alterations different from Russell's, and still others believe the problem lies not in the principles of the theory of classes at all but rather in the underlying logic. The intuitionists are a case in point, complaining that no paradox is forthcoming for the Russell class unless the logical law of the excluded middle is accepted. But that law they reject. More recently some free logicians have joined this group, though eschewing the law of specification but retaining the law of the excluded middle. Indeed, specification, or its equivalent particularization, is crucially involved in the demonstration that the set axiom of comprehension is inconsistent when applied to the Russell class.[10]

The various approaches to the theory of classes in the wake of paradoxes such as Russell's have found counterparts in recent defenders of Meinong's theory of beingless objects. Some, as noted in Chapter 3, alter Meinongian principles in the wake of the threat to the theory latent in putative objects such as the spheroid which is such that it is not a spheroid. Parsons, for instance, as previously noted, rejects the Meinongian principle that the so and so is an object, whatever so and so is, and hence the Meinongian semantic principle that all singular terms refer. The Routleys, on the other hand, seek to retain Meinong's ontological and semantic principles, by challenging the logic licensing the ensuing contradiction. This

[10] Dana Scott, 'Existence and Description in Formal Logic'.

is reflected in their rejection of the logical principle of abstraction, also outlined at the end of Chapter 3.

Why the disparity in Russell's attitude toward classes, on the one hand, and beingless objects, on the other hand? I suspect the anwer concerns utility. When the paradoxes of set theory became known, and some of them were known even to its inventor Georg Cantor, set theory had already been shown to have enormous practical and theoretical use in mathematics. One could recommend dissolution of the realm of classes only at the cost of giving rise to the suspicion that one had completely lost one's mind. Meinong's theory of beingless objects, in contrast, never enjoyed any such advantage. So Russell could with impunity recommend dissolution of the entire realm of such objects at the first sign of paradox. Later work, especially Parsons' *Nonexistent Objects*, suggests that Russell may have been too hasty. A theory of beingless objects has interesting applications in the analysis of fictional objects, dreams, and perhaps most importantly, in the semantics of natural language. Perhaps the applications are not (yet) as spectacular as the applications of the theory of classes, but they are promising enough so that had Russell been aware of them, he might have had second thoughts about beingless objects, and instead might have been led to consider the principles and arguments which led to paradox in cases such as the spheroid which is such that it is not the case that it is a spheroid. This relates to the next general remark.

In the second place, Russell's presumption that statements containing grammatical subjects that refer to no existent precipitate philosophical disaster if treated as predications is simply not well-founded. That presumption has the ring of plausibility if predication is conceived in the manner of the core principle CT, or something like it. But even then, as we have seen, contradiction or similar horrors loom only if the principle of abstraction is accepted. This may be considered a rather extreme defense of the predicational character of (1),

Vulcan is Vulcan,

or

> (17) The spheroid which is such that it is not a spheroid
> is spherical,

but there is nothing correspondingly extreme about the following observation. The concept of predication is not set hard in
cement; predication conceived in the manner of the core principle CT is after all a theory, if a hoary one. However, there is
ample independent reason for concern about that aged party
as was outlined in Chapter 4. If predication is conceived along
the lines of $C\overline{T}$, beingless objects of no kind issue forth without
additional special premises. So even if the complaint against
treating statements such as (17) and/or (1) as predications is
scaled down to the complaint that one is thereby committed to
beingless objects, or at least to beingless objects of a particularly reprehensible kind (however 'reprehensible' is spelled
out), the complaint is ill-founded. The moral of this last observation is that Russell's charge that Meinong's theory founders
on a misconception of the logical form of statements such as
(9)

> The round square is round,

and (10),

> The existent king of France exists,

is a charge which may itself founder on a misconception, a misconception about what predication really is.

Russell's doctrine about the logical form of statements such
as (1) persists, and so does his strategy of paraphrase. This is
so partly because of the profound fear of beingless objects
induced by Russell, a fear that Meinong certainly did little to
dispel. And it is partly because of the great success of Russell's
theory in other areas, some of which are so well outlined by J.
O. Urmson.[11] It is unlikely, therefore, that those who adopt
Russell's theory of the logical form of simple statements con-

[11] See his *Philosophical Analysis: Its Development between the Two World Wars*, Oxford University Press, New York, 1956.

taining expressions such as 'Vulcan', 'the round square', and so on, would be dissuaded of its virtues merely by being shown that beingless objects are nothing to be afraid of, or that treating statements such as (9) and (10) as predications does not commit one to them. The question then arises: leaving aside Russell's arguments that (9) and (10) are not predications, what is wrong with his proposals about what the logical form of those statements really is?

The major and surprising implication is that statements such as (1), (9), and

(18) Ponce de León sought the fountain of youth

all turn out to be false according to Russell's method of paraphrase. The first of these statements, for example, paraphraseable as

There exists exactly one thing which is a planet causing the perturbations in Mercury's orbit,

is false because there exists no such object. The same verdict applies to appropriate Russellian paraphrases of the other two statements.

This state of affairs unsettles many because it collides with deep-seated intuitions. For example, there is the basic intuition that (1) is not only true but logically true. If these intuitions are sustained, a cloud is thereby cast over Russell's conception of the correct logical form of the three statements (1), (9), and (18). A little more than a decade ago Chisholm, using a different example, put the sort of concern over the Russellian paraphrase of (1) this way:

There are some *a priori* statements, according to Meinong, in which nonexistent objects are singled out by means of definite descriptions. 'Not only is the much heralded gold mountain made of gold, but the round square is as surely round as it is square.' What are we to say of 'The golden mountain is golden'? According to Russell's theory of descriptions, some sentences of the form 'The thing which is F is G' may be paraphrased into sentences of the following form: 'There exists an x such that x is F and x is G, and for every (existing) y, if y is

F then y is identical with x.' Hence if we paraphrase 'The golden mountain is golden' in this way, we will have: 'There exists an x such that x is both golden and a mountain, and x is golden, and, for every (existing) y, if y is both golden and a mountain then y is identical with x.' The resulting sentence would seem to refer only to objects that do exist. But is it an adequate paraphrase?

'The golden mountain is golden', according to Meinong, is *true*. But Russell's paraphrase implies 'There exists an x such that x is both golden and a mountain' and is therefore *false*. How can a false statement be an adequate paraphrase of a true one?[12]

Russell, it has to be reported, regarded the alleged failing a positive virtue. In 'On Denoting', he said that 'it is a great advantage' of his theory that simple statements having definite descriptions whose bases are not true of exactly one existing thing are false.[13] Two responses to Russell's 'heroic' attitude come readily to mind. First, one simply cannot be whimsical about the data a theory is supposed to accommodate. Though (one may suppose) there may be degrees of conviction about the truth-values of the three statements above, surely the last of them is beyond question – either that or history has hood-winked us all. So even if one grants that Russell's theory of logical form can withstand the charge that it does not accom-modate the data in the case of (7) – and Meinong certainly would protest – it is strained in the first case, (1), and thoroughly implausible in the last case, (18). Second, if (1), (9), and (18) are really believed to be false, whatever the reason, why indulge in the philosophical overkill of stating that they do not have the logical form of predications? All that is needed to sustain the argument against the principle that

Gs;
So, s has being

is invalid, the principle statements (1)–(18) are alleged to support, is their falsity. It might be responded that there are other independent reasons for maintaining that (1)–(18) are

---

[12] *Jenseits von Sein und Nichtsein*, p. 29.
[13] 'On Denoting', p. 45.

not predications. For instance, if (1),

Vulcan is Vulcan,

is counted false, then the logical principle

RI $s = s$ where the substituends of s are singular terms,

must be rejected on pain of inconsistency. This would require denying that 'Vulcan' is a singular term. But what is the rationale for *that*? Surely not Russell's; that is unacceptable. What then? The answer simply is not forthcoming.

The suggestion that some statements among the three above may not be predications will reemerge shortly. For the moment, grant that they are, and let us look into the final strategy for rejecting the principle of independence. It has, as a matter of fact, just been touched on, though somewhat indirectly. The strategy in question does not challenge the predicational character of the first pair of statements in the list of three above – it holds that they are correctly represented as instances of the form

Gs.

It asserts rather that they are false, and so do not provide cases supporting the invalidity of

Gs;
So, s has being.

Representatives of this approach are now more plentiful than three decades ago. That is because more persons now think that expressions such as 'Vulcan', 'Pegasus', 'The spheroid which is such that it is not a spheroid', and 'The round square' are genuine singular terms. All free logicians do, and even many who are not free logicians. The difference between them concerns the referring status of the four expressions above. No one, except a reform-minded Frege and his disciples, thinks that any of the above expressions refer to subsistent objects, but some free logicians think they all refer, others think that none refer, and still others think only some refer. Terence Parsons, as earlier noted, is one of the latter. He thinks the second and fourth expressions in the list are referential, and the first and third are irreferential.

More importantly, however, is the truth-value status of simple statements containing such singular terms. Here the negative free logician's view is all-important. He considers *all* such statements to be false, and indeed must do so in virtue of the validity of

> *Gs*;
> So, *s* has being,

which he accepts – not surprisingly, because, as explained in Chapter 5, he rejects the principle of independence and its predicational equivalent.

In particular, the negative free logician thinks (1),

> Vulcan is Vulcan,

is false, and also both

> (19) Pegasus is Pegasus,

and

> (20) The round square is the round square.

Indeed, any instance of the schema

> *s* is *s*

where 's' refers to no existent, he holds to be false. Falsehood is also the value he attaches to (9),

> The round square is round.

The credo of the negative free logician is this: *if a statement is a predication it is false if it contains at least one occurrence of a singular term not referring to a subsistent.* And it is often supported by appeal to the dictum that nothing can have no properties.

The idea is this. Pegasus, being nothing, cannot have any properties (or can have nothing truly said of him). Not even self-identity. So (19) must be false. But the doctrine that

nothing can have no properties is not a doctrine that any
Meinongian would deny, even though subscribing to the invalidity of

  Gs;
  So, s has being,

which the negative free logician rejects. How can this be? The
answer is that Meinong does not equate the objects with the
subsistents, but the negative free logician does. For Meinong,
the inference pattern

  Gs;
  So, s is an object

is distinct from the above inference pattern and *is* validating.
Indeed, trivially so because where 's' takes as substituends
singular terms, it has no false instances. So, for him, the
doctrine that nothing has no properties only supports the
validity of inferences of the form

  Gs;
  So, s has being

on the illicit assimilation of the objects to the subsistent
objects; that no nonsubsistent thing has properties is, for the
Meinongian, simply false. Accordingly, those negative free
logicians who support the falsehood of all instances of 's is s',
where 's' takes as substituends singular terms referring to no
subsistent, by appeal to the metaphysical principle that
nothing has no attributes must argue that there are no nonsubsistent objects. In fact, this thesis is seldom ever argued after
Russell. But the plethora of *consistent* theories to the contrary
developed in the last two decades demands such a defense.
The upshot is that the nothing-has-no-properties defense of
the falsehood of, say, (19) lacks force on its own.

   For the sake of argument, let us grant that the Meinongian
doctrine of nonsubsistent objects is wrong. How does the
doctrine of the negative free logician fare then? (The issue is a
real one; for there are many positive free logicians who agree

with the ontological bent of the negative free logician but nevertheless assert the truth of *all* instances of '*s* is *s*'.) Let us resurrect the original list of three statements (1), (9) and (18), and recount why the negative free logician responds in the way he does.

Recall that (1),

Vulcan is Vulcan,

and (9),

The round square is round,

are both counted false because neither Vulcan nor the round square subsists (i.e., the broad sense of 'exists'). On the other hand, (18),

Ponce de León sought the fountain of youth,

would doubtless be counted true, despite there being no fountain of youth. Why? Because this statement is not a predication. The reason? The context '— sought . . .' is non-extensional. That means here that it does not satisfy the principle that coreferential singular terms can be substituted for each other without a change in truth-value. For example, it may be true that

The president sought the dean

and that

The dean is the chairman of the board,

(though the president doesn't know it), but false that

The president sought the chairman of the board.

As was reported in Chapter 4, philosophers of a Quineian bent interpret failure of the principle in question to be evidence that the host statement is not a predication. This explanation suggests a strategy for the negative free logician in other potentially embarrassing cases. Consider, for example,

(21) Sherlock Holmes is a detective.

This statement seems undeniably true. That intuition can now be accommodated by construing the statement in question as short for

(22) In the story by Conan Doyle Sherlock Holmes is a detective,

and noting that contexts of the form

(23) In the story . . .

are notoriously nonextensional. So the original statement, when taken as true, is not really a predication after all, despite its appearance. The general strategy is clear: when the truth threatens, paraphrase it away.

The current paraphrase strategy differs from the Russellian procedure in two ways. First, it does not require that unfulfilled definite descriptions such as 'the fountain of youth' be denied singular termhood, but Russell's procedure does. Second, as far as simple statements are concerned, paraphrase via the non-Russellian method preserves the truth of the paraphrased statement, but Russell's method does not. The goals of the two methods, however, merge in the presence of (18); their common purpose is to establish the nonpredicational character of (18),

Ponce de León sought the fountain of youth.

The non-Russellian paraphrase strategy, nevertheless, is objectionable on various grounds. In the first place, it is a program, not a proven method. This is a point stressed by Terence Parsons in his recent study of nonexistent objects (p. 37). It amounts to an article of faith among those who dread the beingless. In the second place, there is good reason to believe such a method cannot succeed because there are examples which it is implausible to believe can felicitously be paraphrased into nonextensional statements. Consider, for example,

(24) Tom Jones is more ethical than Richard Nixon.[14]

This statement surely is improperly paraphrased as

(25) In the Fielding story Tom Jones is more ethical than Richard Nixon.

Fielding did not know of Nixon, the disgraced United States President, nor was there a character so named in his novel *Tom Jones*. So (25) is false, though (24) is true.

Defenders of the faith could seek to avoid this complaint by declaring (24) really a complex statement, and thus not a counterexample. (The method is intended only to apply to simple statements, i.e., statements containing no logical operator.) The idea is that the comparative 'more ethical than' involves a hidden reference to a given person's morality exceeding the morality of *all* others (including the fictitious Tom Jones) up to some standard. So the original statement contains a suppressed quantifier expression, 'all', and thus is really complex.

This response is interesting; it suggests that no statement containing a comparative can be simple, even statements such as

(26) Prince Charles is taller than Jimmy Carter.

The view has its supporters not only among philosophers but also among linguists.[15] (If the suggestion is rejected, then, of course, the question arises why a comparative statement containing a singular term referring to no subsistent should have a logical form different from one containing no such singular term.)

Even if it be granted that there is a way of adequately paraphrasing comparative statements such as (24), other

---

[14] I heard this asserted at a party one evening in Orange County, California, during the notorious Watergate episode. It was vigorously proposed by a young man in reaction to a Republican dowager's public aversion to the behavior of Tom Jones, the Fielding character of lusty appetite. Orange County Republicans were not known to be equally sensitive about Nixon's actions.

[15] In fact this is just the position of the linguists. J. Bresnan, Syntax of Comparative Clause Construction in English', *Linguistic Inquiry*, 4, (1973) pp. 275–343.

cases threaten the faith in paraphrase. Take, for instance,

(27) Pegasus is fictitious.

This is not a comparative, is true, and is certainly not adequately paraphraseable as

(28) In the myth Pegasus is fictitious,

which is false. If the response is that this shows only that the present paraphrase doesn't work, not that none will, then we are brought resoundingly back to Parsons' point that no argument has ever been given that the current method of paraphrase does work. Sound philosophizing involves more than counterpunching.

III. ARGUMENTS FOR INDEPENDENCE

Defenders of the principle of independence often rest their case on appeal to 'facts' about truth. Meinong thought the truth of a statement such as (9),

The round square is round,

to be a fact as 'hard' as the truth of a statement such as

(29) The earth is round.

Findlay makes the same kind of case at places in his book on Meinong, and it is also the strategy in Chisholm's thoughtful essay 'Beyond Being and Nonbeing'.[16] Usually justification of the principle of independence is the remote purpose. The immediate purpose is proof that there are beingless objects, a conclusion which can be used with other 'facts' to establish the predicational cousin of the principle of independence.

The reasoning, in the terminology of this book, typically follows a pattern rather like this:

Consider the statement

---

[16] *Meinong's Theory of Objects and Values* (2nd edn), and Chisholm in *Jenseits von Sein und Nichtsein.*

(i) The round square is round.

It is surely true. But then it must also be true that

(ii) The general term 'round' is true of what the singular term 'the round square' refers to.

And (ii) cannot be true unless

(iii) the round square is an object.

Now the round square is impossible, and since no subsistent can be impossible, it follows that

(iv) the round square is beingless.

So, the statement

(v) the round square has being

is false. Therefore, the statement (i) does not imply the statement (v).

This pattern of reasoning brings out important hidden assumptions. First, the transition from (i) to (ii) shows that (i) is regarded as a predication in the sense of the core principle CT. Second, it shows that the beinglessness of the round square does not follow from the predicational character of (i) and its truth alone; one must show independently that the object is beingless. Of course, after Frege, in his reformist guise, it is a commonplace that the fact that a traditional predication purportedly about a beingless object is true does not imply that that object is beingless. In Frege's development, as noted in Chapter 5, the object specified by the subject of (i) gets identified with some arbitrarily chosen object which, indeed, subsists. Third, the evidence for the nonsubsistence of the round square plays on its impossible nature, but in other cases – Pegasus or Vulcan, for instance – no such argument is available. It is presumably a 'fact' that they do not subsist.

The upshot of these remarks is this. Defenders of the principle of independence, and its predicational ilk, rely on a lot more than simply the truth of certain statements to accomplish their goals. Moreover, they are not always sensitive to these other assumptions, especially that the statements from which the arguments start are predications, and that the nonsubsistence of the objects of those true predications does not follow from that fact alone. This shows once again that the predicational equivalent of independence does not follow from the predicational character of a statement even in the sense of the core principle CT.

It should also be clear that the argument from the truth and predicational character of, say, (i) in the sense of $\overline{CT}$ to the subsistence of the round square is yet more disconnected, because predication in that sense does not even entail that the round square is an object, let alone a nonsubsistent one.

How do these general considerations apply to specific cases? Consider Chisholm's essay 'Beyond Being and Nonbeing'. He argues that the *prima facie* evidence for Meinong's doctrine of beingless (or 'homeless') objects is the fact that there are all sorts of true statements that 'pertain' to such objects, and that attempts to explain away the *prima facie* appeal to such objects fails. The set of statements he sets the greatest store by are the set of *intentional* statements, statements involving psychological words like 'behave', 'desire', 'think', 'worship', 'sought', and so on. A case in point is the statement

> (30) The thing he fears the most is the same as the thing he loves the most.

Though not specifically considered, no doubt (18),

> Ponce de León sought the fountain of youth,

would also fit into the category of intentional truths Chisholm thinks best supports Meinong's belief in beingless objects.

The problems confronting Chisholm's defense of Meinong's beingless objects by way of intentional statements is threefold. First, as noted recently, such statements are often regarded as nonpredicational, and thus the inference to objects, let alone beingless objects, following the model argument above, cannot get started. Second, if regarded as predications, even in the sense of the core principle CT, the inference to beingless objects requires some independent evidence that the objects are beingless. This has already surfaced in the analysis of the model argument above. Third, though there may be other ways of deducing the beingless objects to which the two intentional statements above 'pertain', Chisholm does not present them. His purpose instead is reflected in the statement: 'It is also reasonable to assume, I think, that Meinong's case will be strengthened to the extent that we find ourselves *unable* to show, with respect to any of these truths, that it need not be construed as pertaining to such objects.'[17] But even if it be granted that the true statements in question cannot be paraphrased away, there is still a lacuna, namely the absence of an argument that gets one from those truths to the beingless objects they are alleged to be about. But considerable doubt has already been raised that any such argument is forthcoming in any straightforward way.

What implications do these considerations have for the predicational equivalent of the principle of independence? The answer is that that principle cannot be justified simply by citing some true statements that are pretty clearly predications even in the strong sense of the core principle CT. That is precisely the moral both of the analysis of model argument and of the above observations on Chisholm's strategy. Essentially the same goes for the similar defense of Meinong's views in Findlay's pivotal book.[18]

Nevertheless, what is sorely needed are arguments, as opposed to linguistic intuitions, that predications containing singular terms that refer to no subsistent are true. This is the key obstacle to adoption of the predicational equivalent of the principle of independence. The soundness of this claim will surface shortly.

The question may be raised: Despite the gap between true predication and beingless object revealed by the analysis of the model argument above, doesn't that argument prove the pre-

[17] *Ibid.*, p. 28.
[18] *Meinong's Theory of Objects and Values* (2nd edn), Chapter II.

dicational equivalent of the principle of independence? For hasn't it been established that (9),

> The round square is round,

is true, that it is a predication, and that the statement

> (31) The round square has being

is false? The answer is: not without question. For though few would deny that (31) is false, others would challenge the presumption that (9) is a predication, and an even greater number would hold it to be false, not true. Let us consider these matters one at a time.

Consider, first, the statements (31),

> The round square has being,

and

> (32) The spheroid which is such that it is not a spheroid has being.

These would be regarded as false by most philosophers whether or not their constituent singular terms are counted referential. The reason, as suggested above, is the principle that

> (33) If s has being, then s cannot be impossible,

where 's' takes as substituends singular terms. This principle seems quite reasonable except perhaps to a stubborn adherent of Russell's *Principles of Mathematics*. That position was examined earlier and found wanting. It is even conceivable that a reformist Fregeian could find it acceptable provided he is willing to regard contexts of the form ' . . . has being' as nonextensional. For suppose the common referent of the grammatical subjects of the two subsistence statements above is some subsisting object, say, the Leaning Tower of Pisa. Then, the falsehood of the specimen statements can be maintained despite the truth of

(34) The Leaning Tower of Pisa has being,

(35) The round square is The Leaning Tower of Pisa,

and

(36) The spheroid which is such that it is not a spheroid is The Leaning Tower of Pisa.

It should be reemphasized that the singular terms replacing '*s*' in (33) can be either referential or *irreferential*; one need not be a Meinongian to accept the falsehood of the two specimen statements (31) and (32). So even if, say,

(37) Pegasus has being

is deemed true, for whatever mystifying reasons, the specimen statements (31) and (32) above are pretty clear examples of falsehoods of being.

The problem now is to find simple statements containing expressions such as 'The round square', 'The spheroid which is such that it is not a spheroid', and the like, such that they are predications and are true. These, seemingly, are readily available. For example, the following new cases seem to qualify:

(38) The winged horse of Bellerophon is the winged horse of Bellerophon;

(39) The man born simultaneously of nine sibling jotun maidens is the man born simultaneously of nine sibling jotun maidens;

(40) The winged horse of Bellerophon is mythological;

(41) The man born simultaneously of nine sibling jotun maidens is mythological.

The pair (39) and (41), it will be recalled, concerns the impossible putative object of Nordic mythology, Heimdal, and the pair (38) and (40) concerns the possible putative object of Greek mythology, Pegasus.

Except in the (discredited) Russellian theory of paraphrase, both of the statements (38) and (39) surely qualify as predications either in some hazy preanalytic sense of 'predication' or in the precise senses of the core principles CT and $\overline{\text{CT}}$. The statements (40) and (41) are not so clearly regarded as predications among non-Russellians, as was intimated at the end of the last section. For though none challenge the truth of each statement in the latter pair, some philosophers – negative free logicians, for instance – challenge the conviction that they are predications in any sense of the word. In a spirit of charity let us grant the negative free logician the point – at least for the moment. (The issue will arise one more time in what follows.) For now we have (38) and (39), irreproachable predications. The question arises then: are they true? No, says the negative free logician, among others. If he is right, these examples would not sustain the predicational equivalent of the principle of independence. But the negative free logician is, I believe, wrong; both the identity statements in question are true.

No one disagrees that were the singular terms in (38) and (39) regarded as specifying even beingless objects, they would be true. For the 2-place general term 'is' being true of *all* pairs of *objects* whose first and second members are the same object would thus be true of pairs of beingless objects of the said kind. Hence either by CT or $\overline{\text{CT}}$, (38) and (39) would be true. Even the negative free logician would assent to this reasoning, but, of course, he denies that the singular terms in question specify anything. They are irreferential in his eyes. So the need for arguments to support the truth of (38) and (39) that don't rely on the assumption that there are beingless objects which the singular terms in question specify.

One such argument is this. According to a long tradition in philosophy a statement of the form

(42) *s* is *t*,

where '*s*' and '*t*' take singular terms as substituends, is true just in case it is true that

(43) Everything *s* possesses is possessed by *t*.

This is, essentially, a version of Leibniz's principle of the identity of indiscernibles, a principle approvingly resurrected in *Principia Mathematica* to explain identity. (The 'is' in '*s* is *t*' is the 'is' of identity.) But if '*s*' and '*t*' are both replaced in (43), first, by 'The winged horse of Bellerophon' and then by 'The man born simultaneously of nine sibling jotun maidens', the result in each case is a logically true statement. Hence, (38) and (39), both of which are instances of (42), would be not only true but logically true. This argument amounts to saying that the logical truth, and hence the truth, of (38) and (39) follows from the very meaning of identity.

Another argument in support of the truth of (38) and (39) utilizes the notion of subsistence entailing predicates, a notion introduced by Henry Leonard in his profound essay, 'Essences, Attributes and Predicates'. Leonard distinguishes between general terms whose occurrence in simple statements is the reason why those statements entail that their constituent singular terms refer to subsistents, and general terms whose occurrence in simple statements licenses no such entailment. An example of the former is the general term 'lives with actual people', and an example of the latter is 'is countable'. What about the 2-place general term 'is' – the 'is' of identity? It falls in the class of general terms not entailing subsistence. The distinction is relevant to the issue over the truth-value of (38) and (39) in the following way.

In contemporary logic the evaluation rule for identity statements, statements of the form (42), is often expressed in this way: a statement '*s* is *t*' is true just in case '*s*' refers to whatever '*t*' refers to. This is relatively uncontroversial. The important question is whether the truth condition just expressed has subsistential (i.e., existential) import. If 'is' is a general term not entailing subsistence, the answer must be no. For if the truth condition did have subsistential import, one could infer that (42) is true only if both *s* subsists and *t* subsists, contradicting the character of the general term 'is' in statements such as (38) and (39). So, again, (38) and (39) turn out to be true. For it follows from the truth condition that

(44) s is s

is always true because 's' refers to whatever 's' refers to.

The negative free logician can be expected to protest that the 'is' of identity is really subsistence-entailing, and hence to object to the argument that the truth condition for statements of the form (42) does not have subsistential import. But this response is open to the objection that whatever use of 'is' the negative free logician is talking about, it is not the 'is' of identity, or at least it is not the 'is' of identity in the sense of the identity of indiscernibles. For, as noted in the preceding argument, that sense of 'is' does not entail the subsistence of the singular terms in the simple statements it is used to compose.

Whatever the ultimate decision about the general term 'is' in (38) and (39), no negative free logician, I venture to say, would contest that the general term 'mythological' is nonsubsistence-entailing. In fact, in virtue of that general term the statements in which it occurs entail the *nonsubsistence* of the purported referents of the constituent singular terms of those statements. But then (40) and (41) must both be true. That verdict is uncontroversial. But because of it the negative free logician can be counted on to respond that (40) and (41) are not predications. Is this really plausible?

We have already seen the required maneuvers applied to simple statements containing the general term 'fictional'. The idea is to paraphrase away simple statements containing the general term 'mythological'. But the candidate

(45) In the myth the winged horse captured by Bellerophon is mythological

is no more acceptable a paraphrase of (40),

The winged horse captured by Bellerophon is mythological,

than

(46) In the story Sherlock Holmes is fictional

is an acceptable paraphrase of

> (47) Sherlock Holmes is fictional.

Some believe that statements such as (40) and (41) can be paraphrased by appeal to the author, creator, or conceiver of the character being described. For example, (47) might be paraphrased as

> (48) Someone (Arthur Conan Doyle) conceived of Sherlock Holmes

and (40) might be paraphrased as

> (49) Someone (or some group) conceived of the winged horse captured by Bellerophon.

Both (48) and (49) are nonextensional, hence not predicational according to the earlier standard. But they are also not acceptable paraphrases of (47) and (40) respectively. In the first place, what we conceive of may turn out to exist – for examples, Pasteur's germs, which his colleagues thought to be merely figments of the imagination. In the second place, if the paraphrase theory were true, then on the common view that mathematical objects are creations of the mind, many mathematical claims would turn out to be nonextensional, though in fact they are not. Thus the extensional statement

> (50) The null set is memberless

turns into the nonextensional

> (51) Someone (Cantor?) conceived the null set to be memberless.

There are many other objections to the paraphrase via psychological verbs procedure not worth recounting here. So the problem again arises: What method of paraphrase is adequate to these and other statements? And we are led back relentlessly to Parsons' observation that the program of paraphrase is more a matter of faith than proven procedure.

A final argument on behalf of the view that some predications containing irreferential singular terms are true is this. Probably some astronomer used 'Vulcan' as shorthand for 'the planet causing the perturbations in Mercury's orbit'. In virtue of this definition the following statement would then be true:

(52) Vulcan is the planet causing the perturbations in Mercury's orbit.

But neither of the singular terms in this predication refers. So the negative free logician is left in the unenviable position of denying that the definition of 'Vulcan' implies (52) or of asserting that (52) implies the subsistence of the objects referred to by the constituent singular terms. The first alternative is counterfactual, conflicting with good practice in mathematics,[19] and the second alternative would reinstitute a version of the ontological argument. For it would then follow from any suitably framed definition of 'God' that he subsists.

To sum up, the weight of the evidence supports the view that there are true predications containing singular terms that specify no subsistent. Attempts to subvert this conclusion rely on unproven procedures at best or clash with informal intuition and facts both of a linguistic or inferential kind and otherwise. The principle of independence is vindicated.

---

[19] It might be suggested that the definition licensing (52) is creative and thus violates 'good practice in mathematics'. The suggestion is that one can infer from (52) a product of the definition of 'Vulcan', that there exists (or subsists) something that is the planet causing the perturbations in Mercury's orbit, something not inferable sans the definition of 'Vulcan'. But this inference goes through only if the underlying logic contains the rule of existential generalization for constant singular terms. In a logic without this rule the definition of (52) is not shown thus to be creative. Whether a definition is creative is always relative to the underlying logic. For example, the definition

R = df the set of sets which are not members of themselves

is quite noncreative in a non-type-theoretical development of set theory provided the rule of existential generalization for constant singular terms is disallowed – as it is in some of Quine's developments of set theory.

IV. A FINAL LOOK AT INDEPENDENCE

The principle of independence has gone through various formulations in this book. The first version, intended to be faithful to Mally's original statement and Meinong's remarks in 'Über Gegenstandstheorie,' is this: the inference

> There are nuclear properties P_1, P_2 ... such that the set of P_1, P_2 ... attaches to s;
> So, s has being

is invalid. The second version, concerning all properties, not just nuclear properties, is the one encountered in other of Meinong's (and Mally's) writings, and is the one most often seen in the authorities. In its simplest form it says: the inference

> There is a property P possessed by s;
> So, s has being

is invalid. It turns out that this version of the principle of independence is equivalent to a certain predicational principle, on the assumption that the principle of abstraction fails – the principle that

> $(\dot{x})$ $(Fx)s$ if and only if Fs

where '$(\dot{x})$ (Fx)' is a general term, 'Fx' is an open sentence, and 's' is a singular term. In its simplest form, that predicational equivalent reads:

> Gs;
> So, s has being

is invalid. There is a certain gain in ontological neutrality with this latest principle. It can be taken as representing an acceptably expressed third version of the principle of independence for those who eschew properties on nominalistic or extensionalist grounds.

In this final chapter most of the discussion has involved what has been variously called 'the predicational equivalent of the principle of independence', 'the predicational cousin of independence', and in the preceding paragraph, 'an acceptably expressed third version of the principle of independence'. The common subject of these three ways of speaking is nevertheless equivalent to the loose (i.e., the second) version of the principle of independence, and that version is the official version on which all the remaining discussion from Chapter 3 onward pivoted. So the principle of independence, in either form, is vindicated. Mally, who subsequently abandoned the 'principle' he invented, was right all the time.

A POSTSCRIPT

ABSTRACTION AND
EXTENSIONALITY

Throughout this book questions have been raised about the logical principle of abstraction – the principle

A $(\dot{x})$ $(Fx)s$ if and only if Fs.

It is truly a fundamental logical principle if ever there was one, and one which, I have argued, Meinong must reject if the reconstruction of the principle of independence, strictly or loosely interpreted, presented in earlier chapters is sound.

In this respect the Routleys have put a finger on a major feature in the logical bases of Meinong's theory of objects. They have argued that by rejecting abstraction, Meinong *can* resist the Russellian challenge that the core principle of predication CT, the principle that all singular terms refer, and the principle that the basis of a definite description is true of the referent of that definite description are jointly inconsistent. I have argued that since abstraction must be rejected by Meinong, the Russellian challenge *is* thereby averted. Something like abstraction is contained in the rules of abstraction and concretion of Quine's early work, 'A System of Logistic'.[1] And something like it is implicit in the often unstated rule of *predicate substitution* in axiomatic versions of standard first order predicate logic.[2] In the current environment of discussion in philosophical logic one cannot afford to be too sanguine about the sanctity of the principle of abstraction. The weight of the growing list of 'refutations' is a threat to the logical conservatism underlying support of that principle. Recall, for example, the intuitive appeal of the complaints leveled against the prin-

[1] Unpublished lectures by Quine, Cambridge, Mass., 1934.
[2] See, for example, Hugues Leblanc, *An Introduction to Deductive Logic,* Wiley, New York, 1955.

ciple in question by Scales, and by Stalnaker and Thomason, in Chapter 3. There may come a time, soon perhaps, when fidelity to the principle of abstraction is counterproductive, when, in other words, the fudging needed to save the principle produces an explanation of logical theory which is more cumbersome than one in which there is outright abandonment of abstraction. To cite a case of such fudging, consider how one might turn aside Scales' objection. It distinguishes between truly denying that Pegasus has the property of existence and falsely asserting that Pegasus has the property of nonexistence. But this supposes that there is no such object as Pegasus. The plausibility of Scales' refutation of the principle of abstraction is overturned simply by rejecting the supposition, and complicating the domains of discourse of logical theory to allow for entities that do not exist. (Score a point for Meinong and Scott!)

If and when the principle of abstraction is consigned to logical oblivion, it should be pointed out that the resulting inelegancies in the apparatus of predicate logic will be offset by clear benefits – at least from certain points of view. An example is the point of view of those who would like to embrace the core principle of predication $C\overline{T}$, but who tremble in anticipation of the scorn sure to issue from their extensionalist colleagues. For the argument that $C\overline{T}$ is nonextensional, in the sense that coextensive general terms substitute *salva veritate*, is thereby averted.

That argument, already presented in Chapter 4, may be further illuminated as follows. Assume a simple predication, containing an irreferential singular term, in the sense of the core principle $C\overline{T}$. The singular term might be 'Vulcan', the general term 'identical with Vulcan', and the predication

(1) Vulcan is identical with Vulcan

or in symbols

(2) $(\dot{x})$ (x is identical with Vulcan) Vulcan,

where the 'is' of predication in (1) is 'symbolized' by the concatenation of general term '$(\dot{x})$ (x is identical with Vulcan)' and singular term 'Vulcan' in (2). On the assumption that 'Vulcan' – the name of the purported planet – is irreferential,

(3) Vulcan is an object

is false, essentially by edict in virtue of the peculiar predicate 'is an object'. Now, no matter what truth-value (1) (or (2)) is assumed to have, in the presence of the principle of abstraction, another statement can be found differing from (2) only by having a general term coextensive with '$(\dot{x})$ (x is identical with Vulcan)' in the place of the latter but which nevertheless differs in truth-value from (2). To illustrate one case, suppose that (2) is false – as the negative free logician would urge. Now notice that the statement

(4) If Vulcan is an object, then Vulcan is identical with Vulcan

is true in virtue of the false antecedent (the conditional, of course, being the classical truth functional conditional). But by A, the principle of abstraction, (4) yields

(5) $(\dot{x})$ (if x is an object, then x is identical with Vulcan) Vulcan

which must also be true. But the general term in (5) is true of exactly the same objects as the general term in (2) – they are coextensive. Clearly if A is rejected, it no longer follows that (5) is true, and the nonextensionality of $C\overline{T}$ is thereby averted. The same holds for the other cases of the argument as detailed in Chapter 4.

The discussion above does not prove that $C\overline{T}$ is extensional; it shows only that a particular proof of the nonextensionality of $C\overline{T}$ does not go through if the principle of abstraction is rejected.

There are various ways to secure the extensionality of $C\overline{T}$ in the sense that coextensive general terms substitute *salva veritate*. For example, one way is to set a statement of the form

$$(\dot{x}) \ (Fx) \ s,$$

true just in case

s is an object and Fs

is true. This amounts to the adoption of a new version of abstraction. Thus, Scales has, in effect, proposed the following modified version of the principle of abstraction in his *Attribution and Existence:*

A1 $(\dot{x}) \ (Fx) \ s$ if and only if s is an object and Fs.

Now note that

$$(\dot{x}) \ (Fx) \ s$$

and

$(\dot{x})$ (if x is an object then Fx) s

are both false – when s is irreferential – in the presence of A1. (When s is referential, no question of nonextensionality arises.) So with A1 the extensionality of $C\overline{T}$ can be secured, though a full proof of the claim would require appeal to Scales' formalization in *Attribution and Existence*. The cost, of course, is that all predications with irreferential singular terms are false, and this will not be palatable to all – van Fraassen and Scott, for instance. There are ways of making $C\overline{T}$ extensional, in the sense used above, which accommodate the conviction that some predications containing irreferential singular terms are true. But enough. The point that rejection of the traditional principle of abstraction, radical and complicating though it is, has its good side, as far as $C\overline{T}$ is concerned, has been made.

Until now it has been maintained that the principle of abstraction holds when the general term is simple (i.e. contains no logical operator), like the general term

$(\dot{x})$ (x rotates)

as opposed to, for example, the general term

$(\dot{x})$ (x rotates and x is in orbit O).

But consider:

(6) Vulcan is the object which vulcanizes

looks true when seen as a product of the Quine-like definition

(7) 'Vulcan' is defined as 'the object which vulcanizes'

but appears false if regarded as attributing a property to the object Vulcan, or, more cautiously, as saying something true of the object Vulcan. If the truth-value of predications is guided by the doctrine that nothing has no attributes, then, on the assumption that 'Vulcan' is not referential,

(8) $(\dot{x})$ (x is the object which vulcanizes) Vulcan

is false. So, it would seem, one might distinguish between (6) and (8). This would suggest that

(9) $(\dot{x})$ (x is the object which vulcanizes) Vulcan if and only if Vulcan is the object which vulcanizes,

an instance of abstraction where the general term is simple – 'is' being thought of as a predicate and not a logical operator – is false.

The theory of general terms has roots in the middle ages. When Frege constructed logic on the model of the theory of functions, the ancient doctrine of general terms received a setback. Such is reflected in A,

$(\dot{x})$ (Fx) s if and only if Fs,

where the 'copula', as reflected in the concatenation of general term and singular term, is given short shrift. Traditional distinctions in the theory of terms, a theory in which Meinong's theory of objects is expressed, are thus obliterated. The distinction between negative general terms and negative statements is an example. The preceding discussion of abstraction suggests that it is time to take a step back from Frege's giant step forward, to survey the thicket, and to look for new paths through it. This, as was urged at the end of the Introduction, is a form of philosophical progress.

BIBLIOGRAPHY

Anderson, A. R., and Belnap, Nuel, Jr., 'Tautological Entailment', *Philosophical Studies*, 13 (1968), pp. 9–24

Belnap, Nuel, 'Questions: Their Presuppositions and How They Can Fail to Arise', in K. Lambert (ed.), *The Logical Way of Doing Things*, Yale University Press, New Haven, 1969

Bencivenga, E., 'Free Semantics', forthcoming

Bressan, Aldo, *A General Interpreted Modal Calculus*, Yale University Press, New Haven, 1973

Burge, Tyler, 'Truth and Singular Terms', *Noûs*, 8 (1974), pp. 309–25

Carnap, R., *Meaning and Necessity*, University of Chicago Press, 1947

Chisholm, R. M., 'Beyond Being and Nonbeing', in R. Haller (ed.), *Jenseits von Sein und Nichtsein*, Akademische Druck-u. Verlaganstalt, Graz, 1972

'Homeless Objects', *Revue Internationale de Philosophie* (1973), pp. 207–23

Chisholm, R. M. (ed.), *Realism and the Background of Phenomenology*, The Free Press, New York, 1960

Church, A., 'Outline of a Revised Formulation of the Logic of Sense and Denotation', Part II, *Noûs*, 8 (1974), pp. 135–56

Findlay, J. N., *Meinong's Theory of Objects and Values*, 2nd edn, Clarendon Press, Oxford, 1963

Frege, G., 'On Sense and Nominatums', in H. Feigl and W. Sellars (eds.), *Readings in Philosophical Analysis*, Appleton-Century-Crofts, New York, 1949

Grandy, R., 'Predication and Singular Terms', *Noûs*, 11 (1977), pp. 163–7

Haack, Susan, *Deviant Logic*, Cambridge University Press, Cambridge, 1974

Kaplan, David, 'Demonstratives', unpublished manuscript, Draft

No. 2, Philosophy Department, UCLA, Los Angeles, 1977

'What Is Russell's Theory of Descriptions?', in W. Yourgrau *et al.*, *Physics, Logic and History*, Plenum Press, New York, 1970

Lambert, Karel, 'Being and Being So', in R. Haller (ed.), *Jenseits von Sein und Nichtsein*, Akademische Druck-u. Verlaganstalt, Graz, 1972

'Existential Import Revisited', *Notre Dame Journal of Formal Logic*, 4 (1963), pp. 288–92

'Impossible Objects', *Inquiry*, 17 (1974), pp. 303–14

'A Logical Reconstruction of Meinong's Theory of Independence', *Topoi*, forthcoming

'On Logic and Existence', *Notre Dame Journal of Formal Logic*, 6 (1965), pp. 135–41

'On the Philosophical Foundations of Free Logic', *Inquiry*, 24 (1981), pp. 147–203

Lambert, K., and Scharle, T., 'A Translation Theorem for Two Systems of Free Logic', *Logique et Analyse*, 40 (1967), pp. 328–41

Leblanc, Hugues, *An Introduction to Deductive Logic*, Wiley, New York, 1955

Leblanc, H., and Thomason, R., 'Completeness Theorems for Presupposition Free Logics', *Fundamenta Mathematicae*, 62 (1968), pp. 125–64

Leonard, H. S., 'Essences, Attributes and Predicates', presidential address, 62nd Annual Meeting of the Western Division of the American Philosophical Association, Milwaukee, 1964

'The Logic of Existence', *Philosophical Studies*, 7 (1956), pp. 49–64

Principles of Reasoning, Dover, New York, 1967

Lewis, C. I., 'The Modes of Meaning', *Philosophy and Phenomenological Research*, 4 (1933–4), pp. 236–50

Linsky, Leonard, 'Frege and Russell on Vacuous Singular Terms', in Matthias Scheru (ed.), *Studies on Frege*, III: *Logic and Semantics*, Friedrich Fromman Verlag, Gunther Holzboog, 1976

Mally, 'Zur Gegenstandstheorie des Messens' (On the Object Theory of Measurement), in A. Meinong (ed.), *Untersuchungen zur Gegenstandstheorie und Psychologie*, Barth, Leipzig, 1904

Meinong, Alexius, 'Gegenstandstheoretische Logik', unpublished MS in the library of the Karl Franzen University, Graz, 1913

Gesamtausgabe (Collected Works), ed. R. Haller and R. Kindinger, Akademische Druck-u. Verlaganstalt, Graz, 1969–78

Möglichkeit und Wahrscheinlichkeit, revised by R. Chisholm, Akademische Druck-u. Verlaganstalt, Graz, 1972

On Assumptions, English translation by James Hearne of *Über Annahmen* (2nd edn), University of California Press, Berkeley, forthcoming

On Emotional Presentation, English translation by M.-L. Schubert Kalsi of *Über emotionale Präsentation* (1917), Northwestern University Press, Evanston, Ill., 1972

On the Theory of Objects, English translation by I. Levi, D. B. Terrell, and R. M. Chisholm of 'Über Gegenstandstheorie', in R. M. Chisholm (ed.), *Realism and the Background of Phenomenology*, The Free Press, New York, 1960

'Selbstdarstellung', in A. Meinong, *Gesamtausgabe*

Über Annahmen, 1st edn, Barth, Leipzig, 1902; 2nd edn, Barth, Leipzig, 1910; also in A. Meinong, *Gesamtausgabe*

'Über Gegenstandstheorie', in A. Meinong (ed.), *Untersuchungen zur Gegenstandstheorie und Psychologie*, Barth, Leipzig, 1904

'Wahrheit und Wahrscheinlichkeit', unpublished MS in the library of the Karl Franzen University, Graz, 1915

Alexius Meinong (ed.), *Untersuchungen zur Gegenstandstheorie und Psychologie*, Barth, Leipzig, 1904

Meyer, R., and Lambert, K., 'Universally Free Logic and Standard Quantification Theory', *Journal of Symbolic Logic*, 38 (1968), pp. 8–26

Parsons, Terence, 'The Methodology of Nonexistence', *The Journal of Philosophy*, 11 (1979), pp. 649–62

Nonexistent Objects, Yale University Press, New Haven, 1980

'Nuclear and Extranuclear Properties, Meinong and Leibniz', *Noûs*, 12 (1978), pp. 137–51

'A Prolegomena to Meinongian Semantics', *Journal of Philosophy*, 71 (1974), pp. 561–80

Posy, Carl, 'Free IPC is a Natural Logic', *Topoi*, forthcoming

Quine, W. V., 'Existence', in W. Yourgrau *et al.*, (eds.), *Physics, Logic and History*, Plenum Press, New York, 1970

Methods of Logic (revised edn), Holt-Dryden, New York, 1959

'On What There Is', in L. Linsky (ed.), *Semantics and the Philosophy of Language*, University of Illinois, Urbana, 1952

Set Theory and Its Logic, Belknap Press of Harvard University, Cambridge, Mass., 1969

'The Scope and Language of Science', in Quine, *The Ways of Paradox*, Random House, New York, 1966

'A System of Logistic', unpublished lectures, Cambridge, Mass., 1934

Word and Object, Wiley, New York, 1960

Rapaport, William, 'Meinongian Theories and a Russellian Paradox', *Noûs*, 12 (1978)

Routley, R., 'On the Durability of Impossible Objects', *Inquiry*, 19 (1976), pp. 247–51

Exploring Meinong's Jungle, Monograph No. 3, Philosophy Department, Australian National University, Canberra, 1980

Russell, Bertrand, *Introduction to Mathematical Philosophy*, George Allen and Unwin, London, 1919

Logic and Knowledge (ed. Robert C. Marsh), Allen and Unwin, London, 1956, and Macmillan, New York, 1956

'On Denoting', *Mind*, NS 14 (1905), pp. 479–93

'On Propositions: What They Are and How They Mean', in *Logic and Knowledge*, pp 285–320

Our Knowledge of the External World, Norton, New York, 1929

'The Philosophy of Logical Atomism', in *Logic and Knowledge*, pp. 175–282

The Principles of Mathematics, 1st edn, The University Press, Cambridge, 1903; 2nd edn, Norton, New York, 1938

Review of A. Meinong's *Untersuchungen zur Gegenstandstheorie und Psychologie* in *Mind*, NS 14 (1905), pp. 530–8

Ryle, Gilbert, 'Intentionality – Theory and the Nature of Thinking', in R. Haller (ed.), *Jenseits von Sein und Nichtsein*, Akademische Druck-u. Verlaganstalt, Graz, 1972

Scales, Ronald, *Attribution and Existence*, University of Michigan Microfilms, Ann Arbor, 1969

Schock, Rolf, *Logics Without Existence Assumptions*, Almqvist and Wiksell, Stockholm, 1978

Scott, Dana, 'Advice on Modal Logic', in K. Lambert (ed.), *Philosophical Problems in Logic*, Reidel, Dordrecht, 1969

'Existence and Description in Formal Logic', in R. Schoenman (ed.), *Bertrand Russell, Philosopher of the Century*, Allen and Unwin, London, 1967, and Atlantic, Little Brown, New York, 1967

Skyrms, Brian, 'Supervaluations: Identity, Existence, and Individual Concepts', *The Journal of Philosophy*, 16 (1968), pp. 477–83

Stalnaker, R., and Thomason, R., 'Attribution in First-Order Modal Logic', *Theoria*, 3 (1968), pp. 203–7

Suppes, P., *Introduction to Logic*, Van Nostrand, New York, 1957

Thomason, Richmond, *Symbolic Logic*, Macmillan, New York, 1970

Twardowski, K., *On the Content and Object of Presentations*, translated by R. Grossmann, Martinus Nijhoff, The Hague, 1977

Urmson, J. O., *Philosophical Analysis: Its Development Between the Two World Wars*, Oxford University Press, New York, 1956

Van Fraassen, Bas, 'Presupposition, Supervaluations and Free Logic', in K. Lambert (ed.), *The Logical Way of Doing Things*, Yale University Press, New Haven, 1969

Van Fraassen, Bas, and Lambert, Karel, *Derivation and Counterexample*, Dickensen, Encino, Ca., 1972

Whitehead, A., and Russell, B., *Principia Mathematica*, 2nd edn, Cambridge University Press, Cambridge, 1925

INDEX

absolute idealism, 9, 39, 131
abstraction, principle of,
    and extensionality, 159–63
    and predication, theory of, 52–5, 60,
        61, 62, 67, 116, 136, 157
Aristotle, 11, 14

being,
    and being determined, 25–6
    and existence, 4–5, 5n–6n, 9, 13–14,
        14n–15n, 16–21, 18n, 26, 26n, 30
    the 'is' of, 32–3
    and nonbeing, 4, 14–21, 19n, 21n, 26–
        7, 123–9; as properties, 18–21, 31
    not independent of nature of object,
        24–8
    Plato on, 126–7
    see also independence; subsistence
beingless objects, xv, 2, 5, 8–10, 14–18,
    25n, 26n, 27, 34n, 36, 62, 63, 64, 65n,
    76, 134–56
    fictional objects as, 17–18, 32, 136
    and free logic, 97–8, 142–3, 152, 154,
        156
    and independence, principle of, 9–10,
        18, 55–6, 56n, 121, 146–8
    Meinong's defence of, 15–18
    and Meinong's theory of predication,
        xv, 63, 64–5, 67–8
    and the nature of objects, 17, 20–1, 31
    and noncontradiction, principle of,
        34n, 46, 47–8, 56–60, 131–2, 134,
        135, 136–7
    and psychological discourse, 3, 36–8,
        148–9
    and quantification, 5, 15n, 97
    reference to, 8, 34n, 35–6, 55–6, 62, 63,
        64, 152, 154, 156
    Russell's criticism of, 33n–34n, 46–8,
        56–8, 62, 68, 130, 131–2, 134, 135,
        136–9, 142, 159

virtual classes as, 8–9, 98n
Bencivenga, Ermanno, 90
Bolzano, B., 100–2
Bradley, F. H., 9
Brentano, F., 12, 13, 37, 38
Bressan, Aldo, 70
Burge, Tyler, 69n, 78, 79, 80, 88, 90, 91,
    92, 111, 118–21

canonical language, 2–3, 76, 101–2
Cantor, Georg, 136
Carnap, R., 43, 64, 70, 83
Castañeda, Hector, 4
Castell, Aubrey, xiii
Caulkins, Mary, 109
Chisholm, R. M., 4, 21n, 29, 37n, 138–9,
    146, 148–9
classes, theory of, 135, 136
    and existence, 8–9
contextual definitions, 8
contradiction, see noncontradiction

defective objects, 31, 63, 64
definite descriptions, 33n, 42, 46, 47, 63,
    67, 81, 100, 102, 114, 130, 132–5,
    138–9, 144, 159
definition,
    contextual, 8
    creative, 156n
    theory of, and free logic, 104
Descartes, René, 30–1

equivocation, 108
evaluation rules,
    for identity statements, 153–4
    and the logical form of predication, 43,
        73, 75–84, 87–8, 92–3
excluded middle, 135
existence, 57n, 75
    and being, 4–5, 5n–6n, 9, 13–14, 14n–
        15n, 16–21, 26, 30

and classes, 8–9
as nonextensional, 81, 81n
and objects, 5n–6n, 23
as a property, 57n, 113
existential generalization, 107, 114–15,
    156n; *see also* quantification
'exists' as a predicate, 3, 5n–6n, 81, 113–
    14
and free logic, 113–14
extensionality, principle of,
    and abstraction, principle of, 159–63
    and objectivity, 87
    and predication, 63, 64–6, 70–1, 81,
        85n, 87, 157, 160–2

fictional objects, *see under* objects
Findlay, John, 4, 7–8, 19, 20, 21n, 25n,
    58–9, 63, 65, 71–2, 146, 149
Fine, Kit, 8
free logic, xv, 15n, 56, 58, 59, 79–80, 94–
    122, 135
and beingless objects, 97–8, 142–3,
    152, 154, 156
definition of, 105
and existence assumptions, 105–13,
    123
and general terms, 105, 113, 115–21,
    123, 154
and identity, 35, 106, 116–18, 120,
    141–3, 152, 154, 161
and independence, principle of, xv, 10,
    35–6, 90–1, 94, 98, 115–22, 123, 141
misunderstandings about, 107–15
motivations for, 98–104
negative, 35n, 116, 117–18, 120, 141–4,
    152, 154, 156, 161
neuter, 116
and ontology, 111–12, 121–2
positive, 35–6, 116, 117–18, 119, 120,
    121, 142–3
and predicate logic, 110–11
and predication, xv, 10, 68–9, 77–8, 80,
    90–1, 115–21, 152, 154
and quantification, 15n, 104, 105, 106–
    7, 114–15, 121
and singular terms, *see under* reference
of singular terms; singular terms
universally, 109
Frege, Gottlob, xv, 10, 59, 63, 65, 72, 83,
    87, 95–6, 111, 116, 140, 150, 163
on predication, 40, 41, 46–7, 49, 76, 94,
    147
on scientific language, 40, 41, 46–7,

76n, 116
on singular terms, 46–7, 59, 76, 95–7,
    116, 140

general terms, 30, 40, 42n, 67, 99–100,
    104, 153–4, 160–3
and abstraction, principle of, 52–3, 54–
    5, 61–2, 160–3
comprehension of, 64, 65
distension of, 63–4, 66
extension of, 64–6, 84–5, 160–2
and free logic, 105, 113, 115–21, 123,
    154
and incomplete objects, 71, 73
intension of, 64, 65
and logic not free of existence assump-
    tions, 105
and predication, theory of, 43–5, 61–2,
    71, 77, 78, 80–3, 125–6
and truth-value, 45, 47–8, 49–50, 62,
    70, 71, 77, 78, 82–3, 85–7, 115–21,
    147
Grandy, Richard, 69n, 118–20

Haack, Susan, 111
Hegel, G. W. F., 9, 11, 131
Hume, David, 11

idealism, absolute, 9, 39, 131
identity, 69n, 106, 116–18, 128–9, 131–
    43, 147, 150, 151–4, 160–1
and free logic, 35, 106, 116–18, 120,
    141–3, 152, 154, 161
the 'is' of, 69n, 131, 153–4
identity of indiscernibles, 153, 154
impossible objects, 6n, 10, 15, 20, 34n,
    58–60, 61, 62, 67–8, 74–5, 147,
    151–2
incomplete objects, 26n, 71–4
independence, principle of, xi–xvi, 9–11,
    18, 21n, 23n, 25n, 29n, 36n, 157–8
arguments against, 126–46
and beingless objects, 9–10, 18, 55–6,
    121, 146–8
defended, 146–56
and free logic, xv, 10, 35–6, 90–1, 94,
    98, 115–22, 123, 141
and indifference, principle of, xv, 18–
    21, 19n, 31–2
logical nature of, 23–36
and objects, 13–18
and predication, theory of, xiii, xv–xvi,
    10, 32–6, 39–42, 49–53, 55–6, 61,
    73–4, 88–93, 94, 115–21, 123–6,

For EU product safety concerns, contact us at Calle de José Abascal, 56–1°, 28003 Madrid, Spain or eugpsr@cambridge.org.

www.ingramcontent.com/pod-product-compliance
Ingram Content Group UK Ltd.
Pitfield, Milton Keynes, MK11 3LW, UK
UKHW012343130625
459647UK00009B/503